A gift from
The Friends of the
Saint Paul Public Library

Also by James Carville

*. . . And the Horse He Rode In On*

*We're Right, They're Wrong*

*All's Fair* (with Mary Matalin)

# Stickin'

### The Case for Loyalty

# James
# Carville

SIMON & SCHUSTER • New York  London  Sydney  Singapore

SIMON & SCHUSTER
Rockefeller Center
1230 Avenue of the Americas
New York, NY 10020

SIMON & SCHUSTER and colophon are registered trademarks
of Simon & Schuster, Inc.

Designed by Bonni Leon-Berman

Manufactured in the United States of America

10 9 8 7 6 5 4 3 2 1

Library of Congress Cataloging-in-Publication Data is available.

ISBN 0-684-85773-1

# Acknowledgments

**I acknowledge everybody who** has helped me in my life; cared for me; loved me. They are too numerous to mention. You know who you are; I know who you are, and that is the most important thing.

I do want to acknowledge Ian Jackman, who sweated with me, read with me, listened to me, traveled with me, wrote for me, ate with me, and helped me put this book together.

To my sister Mary Anne Olivier,
whose loyalty, love, and sense of decency know no bounds

# Contents

# Stickin'

# Introduction

**When you are as** outspoken as I am, and you dish it out a little, you have to be able to take it when someone takes a swipe at you in the press. I've been called a lot of things in my time. To name a few, I've been called a court jester, a clown, a comedian, serpent head, gamecock, a slimy little worm, a hatchet man, an attack master, and a bottom-feeder. For some reason animals, and particularly dogs, tend to suffer in comparison to me: I've been called a rabid dog, an attack dog, an aggressive pit bull, a junkyard dog, a presidential Doberman, and a political rottweiler. I'm called a totalitarian, a loyalist, a foul-mouthed bore, a hack, and a sight to behold. And instead of saying "Carville said such-and-such," people write that I "spew," "snipe," "crow," and "froth."

Now, I am a grown man and I don't mind most of this. Some of the labels I find funny and get a kick out of, like when I'm described as "the aging enfant terrible in midlife crisis" or "the charismatic love child of Danny DeVito and Mr. Clean." Some of the labels even come from a member of my own family. And others come from the most venerable and reputable of sources. I was called a "buffoon" in the paper of record, the *New York Times*, and the *Washington Post* described me fondly as "Clinton's gunsel,* his button man, the odious James Carville."[1] I am proud of these distinctions.

---

*Whatever the hell that is. I'm sure I am one, I just don't know what it is.

Amidst all of these insults is the word "loyalist." These days the word "loyal" and its variations is used as the coup de grâce of insults, as if to point out a weakness of mind or character. Or it's used when they can't think of anything good to say— "yes, but he is very loyal." You know what I'm talking about.

Now why is this? At what point in history have we gotten to where loyalty is not a positive thing, where it is not valued? To me, it's key—loyalty is one of the essential attributes a person must have and must demand of others. Now you may think the old Cajun's just Ragin' again, but I'm serious, and I think there's something badly wrong with what I see around me. Where I come from and what I believe strongly in is that loyalty, though a complicated and many-splendored thing, is still a virtue. In history and in literature, the snitch has always been a comic or pathetic figure, so when did the snake-in-the-grass become so revered and the tittle-tattle so venerated? Why is nothing more beloved than a turncoat?

I think we can look to the nation's capital for a clue. Nowhere in the entire world is disloyalty more rewarded and rewarded well than in Washington. There is simply no faster way for you to join the ranks of Washington society or the media elite than by running to the press with a backstabbing story—and recently, it's no secret, that means you need to be a rabid Clinton-hater. Heck, if Brutus lived today, there would be a monument to him on the Mall. If you go on television to say something negative, hateful, and Clinton-bashing, by God your mailbox will be filled with black tie invites and requests for cable television appearances.

I think the problem is at its worst in Washington and this is where we must tackle it head-on. To some extent, disloyal, unprincipled backstabbers are encouraged by a media Beast that can't get enough treachery and deceit in its diet. What I call the Commentariat is sneaking around all the time trying to smell a rat so they can interview it on background. The Beast has to be fed, and there are plenty of people with conflicting kinds of agendas shooting off their mouths. It's a difficult enough place to do business without having to worry about watching your back every minute of the day.

Until I started being called "loyal" in the media, and started getting letters about it, I'd never really thought that much about my sense of loyalty one way or the other. If someone is going to be calling you something, it might behoove you to think about it a bit. Gamecock and Doberman I can figure out, but loyal is something else. So I thought about it a bit and this book is the result. Some people came up to me and said, "I don't agree with Clinton, but I admire the way that you stuck with him." This is the way most people talk about this, so I'm going to call my book *Stickin'*.

As it turns out, loyalty looks pretty simple on the face of it. Setting yourself aside, sticking has to start with the family, right? I'm from a big family, the oldest of eight children, and the first thing you learn is, you don't go and rat on your siblings to your parents. That's basic. You're loyal to your brothers and sisters and to your family as a whole. The stickin' starts at home and you take it from there.

That sounds pretty simple, yes? Well, it's really not so easy.

Dogs are famously loyal—and that's probably one of the "negative" connotations of calling someone a junkyard dog. I have three dogs and they're very loyal to me, but that's not real loyalty; that's obedience. Nor is it the "omertà" stuff you see in Mafia movies. People don't seem to appreciate that there's a difference between being loyal and being a sycophant or an idiot. The sycophant has an easy job. He or she just determines who's in power and then sucks up to them. In our campaigns we had a name for a sycophant: "Ditto." "Ditto" is not being loyal, that's being an opportunist. (Ditto Boland was a character in *The Last Hurrah* by Edwin O'Connor, which, in my opinion, ranks second only to *All the King's Men* as a political novel.)

And an idiot's just an idiot.

Genuine loyalty has to be based on something substantial. To begin with, you have to be true to yourself and your own principles—who could disagree with that? But is loyalty one of your principles? That's the question. (I'm not saying that principles are never applied in Washington. People resign "on principle" all the time. But for the life of me, I can't recall hearing about someone in a tough spot who *stayed* out of principle.)

Where loyalty comes into play is through difficulty. Loyalty not taxed is really not loyalty. If you loan a friend money you know you're going to get back, that's not a demonstration of loyalty, that's an investment. If you loan them money and you hope you get it back—that's loyalty.

There's a quote about this that has been attributed to a bunch of people. One version has a politician saying to the nineteenth-century British prime minister Lord Melbourne, "I will support you as long as you are in the right." To which Melbourne said, "That is no use at all. What I want is men who support me when I am in the wrong." (Some say Sam Rayburn said it. Others, Earl Long, governor of Louisiana. I am loyal to my home state, so I give credit to Earl Long. It's a good line; maybe they all said it.)

Now I really believe people in America have a yearning to stick with something. They themselves want to stick with someone, or see others stand up for somebody even when they are wrong once in a while rather than stabbing them in the back. The world can be a harsh and lonely place and you need something you're connected to. So we need to step back here and look at what does connect us.

It's easy to see that we are quickly becoming a less rooted society. Not so many years ago, three and four generations of families lived together and looked after each other from cradle to grave. Like in Carville, Louisiana, where I grew up and where my great-grandmother was the postmistress (oops, maybe I should have said "postperson"), and my grandfather and father were postmaster. There, an entire family lived in what is now the same zip code. Nowadays people are more mobile and families break up and move apart. You'll go to college out of state and move to the city to find a job. And when you are employed you'll find that companies don't hire people for life anymore—they "outsource" and hire temps and the like. One half of all jobs last less than one year.

If you do go back to your hometown, you probably won't recognize it. The corner stores are gone and there's a mall where the park used to be. You don't even have to go to a book-store any more, let alone a library.

My family used to run a country store in Carville. We were definitely aware of the people that shopped there and the people that didn't. Over time, you develop relationships with local merchants and the tradespeople who work out of your hometown, so if something goes wrong, people are more inclined to take care of you. They help you and you help them. You stick together.

In the Shenandoah Valley where we live now, we try to trade with the smaller, local stores. I usually go to Ken's True Value Hardware store. They can help you find whatever thingumijig or whatyoumicallit you need. At one of those giant mall stores, lots of luck. There's a level of friendliness and service there that takes me back to our country store in Carville.

But I feel we've moved away from that type of living, and we've lost the sense of community that was its greatest benefit. There are busted connectors all over the place. The everyday stuff that we had in common often isn't there anymore. People stay in touch by e-mail. I have as much chance of turning on a computer as I have of flying a 747. And e-mail's not a real con-nection to me. It's words on a screen.

I do think you need a group of relationships so you can live and thrive. You need things that you feel you belong to. Things you want to stick with. I think Washington has it wrong: People really do want to reconnect to places and each other. And people respect someone who sticks with someone or something through rough times. Or, as Barry Goldwater might say, opportunism at the expense of loyalty is no virtue. What I want to try to do is make a case for loyalty for all the people who want to stick with things.

But as I said, it isn't easy. People are going to have conflicting loyalties and there are no absolutes we can point to as moral guidelines that must be followed. It's not a 100 percent thing. Also, it's easy to see that you can be extremely loyal to something bad. Loyalty is not a virtue when it is misapplied—I'm sure a lot of Nazis thought they were very loyal people. Nor do I want to set myself up as an icon of loyalty. I'm not writing this book because I am a shining example of a loyal person, because I'm not sure that I am. I can think of times in my life that I've betrayed or let down people I shouldn't have.

What we are going to be able to say is that untested loyalty is just a bromide. For it to be meaningful, you have to put something at risk. We are going to talk about different things that we are loyal to. We are even going to delve into a few things out of literature and a fine book on loyalty written by, believe it or not, a Columbia University law professor.

By and large this is a book about stickin', and we are going to try to stick to the simple things and some of the things that you are going to confront in your life. If you stick with me in this book, we'll try to get into some lively things about this subject. And for those of you who have stuck with me in the past and bought my other books, you know that you will get a recipe or two, a few anecdotes, and not a lot of highfalutin philosophizing.

# Why I Stuck with Bill Clinton

**Throughout the whole period** that the president was being investigated, on occasions too numerous to count, people would approach to give me an opinion. They'd come up to me on street corners, in hotel lobbies, in airports, just about any where, and they'd say: "Man, you are really out there for Clinton." Some people liked that fact; some people said, "I don't agree with you, but I like the way you have stuck with your guy"; and others didn't like it from any perspective. Some of these people thought I was just being a sycophant or they thought Bill Clinton had a picture of me with a sheep or something. But on the whole, I think a majority of the comments were favorable. And everyone did seem to have an opinion one way or the other about my vigorous defense of the president.

Some friends of mine thought that I should put a little distance between me and the president, or at least get a little wiggle room. I didn't know where this was going to end, they would tell me, and I didn't want to be on the wrong side of history. People are going to look at you and think you are just sucking up. I think my friends were well intentioned. I was an older parent with one young girl and another kid on the way, and they were thinking of the long term. But I rejected their advice.

Up to now, I've never really had the opportunity to explain to people how it got to be that I was the guy sitting on *Meet the Press* or *Larry King Live* or *Crossfire* defending the president. So what I thought I'd do first here is answer the question: Why did I stick with Bill Clinton?

I think it's important to put what I did in context. It just didn't spring up one day. There was Bill Clinton; here was James Carville, and James Carville defended Bill Clinton. You have to go back and learn a little bit about where I came from and how my relationship with Bill Clinton was forged. And you have to look at what I felt I owed him, and what I felt had been done to him.

I grew up sixty-five miles north of New Orleans in Carville, Louisiana, a place on the river they used to say was so far in the sticks you had to pipe sunshine in. This is a hard thing to conceptualize perhaps, particularly in the America of today, but I actually grew up loving politics. Even as a little boy, I was fascinated by it. It might have been an odd thing for a kid, but I liked the excitement, and back in Louisiana in the mid-1950s, politics was very colorful. I would mimic the more flamboyant politicians much the way other kids mimicked entertainers or musicians.

I can vividly remember being a runner for the Fidelity National Bank in downtown Baton Rouge. (I got a job there as a result of my grandfather being on the board of directors—a

**If you** think the impeachment business was an awful thing to live through, let me tell you something. Nineteen ninety-eight was going great for me until January. Then the whole thing started and I couldn't sleep; I wasn't eating. I was tense and jumpy every time the phone rang. One night I was tossing and turning and all my fidgeting woke Mary up. She'd finally had enough and said, "I don't really care what happens to your client, but I do care what happens to you and you have got to do something. You've got one young child and another on the way and you've got to figure out a way to take care of yourself. You're not going to get through it emotionally, mentally, or even physically if you keep going at the rate you're going now."

She was right. My beautiful wife knows me well and could tell where this was going if I didn't get a hold of it. I thanked her and went downstairs so she could get some sleep and I could think about it. We were about a week into this thing and I could tell by the hurricane force of the coverage and the glee in the eyes of the independent prosecutor and his team of legal Dobermans that this wasn't going away without a struggle.

And I thought about it and made my coffee and went back up in the morning. Mary said, "What are you going to do?" I think she was going to encourage me to seek some kind of professional help or something, but I said, "I've got this thing figured out. I've got three things I am going to do to get through this. First, I am going to keep my sense of humor because that is what has served me well; secondly, I am going to fight like hell; and thirdly, I am going to try not to call anyone an MF on television."

lesson in loyalty here, or, should I say, just plain old nepotism.) I was fourteen years old and one of my assignments was to run stuff over to the State Capitol. I loved going there. I was totally fascinated by the legislature, by the ringing of the bells and crash of the gavels, by the smell of the printer's ink and the cigar smoke. It was my version of the theater.

I dreamed about being a part of the place but never really did very much about it. I did some work for people running for the state legislature. I would help put some signs up and, maybe just as often, tear the other guy's signs down. I'd distribute literature and generally help with the campaigns. But I never really figured on making a life of it.

After an undistinguished academic career and a stint in the Marine Corps, where I attained the rank of corporal (hence half the reason for my self-assigned moniker of Corporal Cue Ball), I went to law school. I was an okay law student—I wasn't law review or in the top 10 percent of the class or anything like that. I started practicing law in Louisiana and I was, quite frankly, less than a mediocre lawyer.

One day, when I was thirty-seven years old, I was sitting at my desk, looking out the window. I thought to myself, If I had to hire a lawyer, I wouldn't hire me. So I'm not going to ask anyone else to. I went into my boss's office and quit.

I don't think the people I was practicing law with were very sorry to see me leave. But they said, "What are you going to do?" I said, "All my life I've wanted to be a political consultant and I'm going to take off and try to do it. I'm single. If I don't try it now, I'm just never going to do it."

And as the result of the intervention of Peter Hart, who helped get me a job running a Senate campaign in Virginia, and with the encouragement of Mark Shields, who is now a nationally syndicated columnist and co-host of *The Capital Gang*, I set off on a career as a political consultant. Both of these men remain my dear friends.

I had a very slow start in my new profession. The Senate campaign in Virginia was the first experience I had outside of Louisiana and we lost. Next I got work running a Senate race in Texas and we lost that race too. So I was forty years old and I was 0-for-2.

I reached a pretty low point in my new career. I was in Washington, D.C., on Massachusetts Avenue, Northeast, and I will never forget what happened. I had all the clothes I owned in a garment bag. At this time, I was knocking on doors looking for a job. If any of you have ever done this, you know what I'm talking about. I'd be told, "Mr. so-and-so's in but he can't see you. He's kind of tied up." I'd sit and wait for three hours. People wouldn't take my phone calls. I was begging and scrapping and I couldn't get anyone to see me or take my telephone call.

So I was standing on Massachusetts Avenue. It was late March or April. It was cold. It was raining real hard. And the strap on my garment bag broke. Everything I owned ended up in a mud puddle. I sat down and started crying. I was forty-one years old and I was a broken man. I had no money, no health insurance, nothing. I was close to having to crawl back to Louisiana and ask somebody to take me in and give me some make-work. Remember Blanche DuBois in *A Streetcar Named*

*Desire?* She went to live off the kindness of strangers; I was going to have to live off the generosity of my friends. I was going to have to go home to admit failure.

But the last thing that dies in somebody is a dream. You can be a broken person, but as long as your dream is intact you'll keep going. And somehow, I kept it together. Months later, someone told me about a guy running for the office of governor of Pennsylvania. They said he had run three times and he had lost three times. He couldn't find anyone to run his campaign. Like the two ugliest people in the class the night before the prom, we just kind of stuck with each other. It was 1986 and the man was Bob Casey. We worked hard and we won that race.

Life started picking up for me a little bit. I got my first credit card. In nineteen hundred and eighty-seven, when I was forty-three years old, I qualified for a credit card for the first time. I was working at what I wanted to be doing and, all told, I was a happy man.

But in the political business there's one office that overshadows everything else and that's president of the United States. Not everyone knows who ran the governor's race in California or the Senate race in New York, but everyone knows the people who work in presidential politics. It's the gold, the silver, and the bronze. That's the big show and you're always waiting for the call.

In 1991 I got a phone call from a dear friend, a man who, years later, basically married Mary and me, the governor of Georgia, Zell Miller. He said, "I've got a man here running for president that I want you to talk to. He's the governor of Arkansas." So I got on the phone with Bill Clinton. We met and I thought he was a nice enough man. I thought this was a man I could work with. So I went to work for Bill Clinton on December 1, 1991. I was one of four or five people on the campaign, a general consultant.

We go through the primaries and we have our ups and downs. I had a pretty good job on the campaign in Little Rock. I got to go to meetings and if I said something, people took what I said seriously, even if they didn't always do what I said. But life was going pretty well for me when I compare it to where I had been. I was cruising along; I had a little money in the bank. Things were not too bad at all.

In late May or early June 1992, I got a call. The governor and Mrs. Clinton wanted to see me in the mansion. I wondered what they wanted but figured it was a big meeting of some kind. I drove over to the mansion and walked in and sat down. And they walk in and it's just the two of them, the governor and Mrs. Clinton. There's three of us sitting at a table.

The governor said, "James, we've been thinking, and what we want you to do is to take over the campaign."

What?

Now right there, seven years after everything I owned was lying in a mud puddle in the middle of a street in Washington, D.C., I was being given the biggest job in the entire world of political consulting. Nothing else is even close. And that's the opportunity these people gave me. They put it right in my lap. I was dumbfounded and then I was terrified, and I went back to the office and worked my ass off for them. But I never forgot the trust they placed in me.

I was the first person to eat with the Clintons after the election. It was just the three of us. A bowl of vegetable soup, a tuna sandwich, and iced tea with the sugar already in it (we were still in Arkansas). It was an incredibly nice gesture. They asked me what I wanted to do with my life, and they thanked me for the great job I did. We shook hands. I hugged the president and kissed Mrs. Clinton and left. Eventually I went to work for myself, but I never, ever forgot what these people did for me.

Over the years I developed a personal relationship with the president. He would call me if something big or tragic happened in my life. He called my mother from time to time. He did the kinds of things that friends do for each other. I'm not going to say my best friend in the entire world was the president of the United States, but he was a friend of mine. He and his wife still are friends of mine.

So my friends went to the White House. And the next thing you know, they started the investigations. There was the FDIC investigation, the RTC investigation, the independent counsel. They spent $20 million, $25 million. There were hundreds of investigators: lawyers, special prosecutors, FBI agents, private detectives. They subpoenaed every tax return the Clintons had filed for thirty years, every check, every scrap of paper. They unleashed the entire power of the Establishment on them—not only the federal legal establishment, but the Washington press establishment, too. They found people who were in business with the Clintons and they started squeezing them and asking them for anything they had. "Give us anything and we'll let you go."

I was watching this and things were going great for me, let me tell you. That first Tuesday in November, I had gone to bed an ordinary person, and I had woken up the next morning a genius. James Carville was suddenly the smartest person you had ever met in your life. They were making movies about me. I was getting all kinds of money to write books and make speeches. I would walk into a restaurant it takes most people three months to get into. They'd kick someone out and say, "Get out of here, you rube, that's Mr. Carville's seat. Get this man what he needs." I went to California and movie stars and God knows who would call me. Everything was wonderful for me. Everything was just great.

But I could not sit by and do my thing and just watch what was happening. These people were friends of mine. I mean, they took the president's wife down to the grand jury and I thought they were going to put her in jail. They drove the president into a legal debt of millions of dollars. They leaked all sorts of half-baked facts and accusations to the press.

And five years and $50 million later, Eureka. We got him. SEX!

**On August 17,** the day the president testified, his wife called me and asked me to come down to the White House. I sat down next to her and she held my hand. She said, "James, I don't know how we're going to get through this, can you continue to help us?"

I said, "Yes, ma'am. I can help you."

I would have been a big person in Washington if I'd turned my back on them. There would have been a nice column about me, saying that I was a person of great integrity. The Sunday morning crowd would have said, "Carville exhibits a refreshing independence. He's not under the yoke of the White House anymore. He's speaking his mind." I would have been the toast of Washington for about a week, but then I would have had to live with myself. And after everything was done and they'd all gone home, years later I would still have had to live with myself.

So I did what I had to do. I really don't apologize for it. I think the president is a good man who did a bad thing and he's entitled to a defense. If I played any small role in defending a good man who has done more for this country than the last two presidents combined—let alone what he did for me personally—then I am truly honored. And what he had done for me was give me my opportunity of a lifetime and become my friend.

We say that loyalty has to be tested. But in this case, when it came down to it, I decidedly did not think that this was a tough test. Bill Clinton is a friend. He's a good man and he has a good heart. He's not a perfect man, but he is a good man and a great president. When I call someone "good" I don't do it lightly—that's not something I sling around. So let me say it again: This decidedly was not a very difficult question for James Carville to answer. I did not feel tested in any way by that. I did not have to anguish or agonize very long over that decision. It's clear that in my world, you don't abandon a guy over sex. You stick with him.

I don't feel I owe people a justification for doing what I did, but I do feel that in a book on loyalty, an explanation is in order. In the end, sticking with the president does not make me a really loyal person. But had I not done this, I would have been a backstabber of the first order.

When all is said and done, it is the law of the playground that applies. You mess with my friend, I'm coming after you. It was an instinctive obligation that I felt. It has nothing to do with the intellectual posturing, the pontificating, or anything else. When you've been unsuccessful your first forty-eight years and you hit the lottery your forty-eighth, you're not likely to change.

I did what I knew I had to do. I had to stick with my friend. It was never really that close a call for me.

**At the height** of the Starr fiasco, around January 1999, I was getting a lot of mail and a lot of questions from people. One of the questions I would get most often would come along these lines. I would be giving a speech and someone, generally a woman, would say to me, "You know, Mr. Carville, I saw you on *Meet the Press* with your wife and two children and I've got to tell you you've got gorgeous young girls. I'm sure you've thought about this, but these girls are not going to be young forever.

"They're going to read about all of this, and not just about Bill Clinton. They're going to read about their Daddy and what he did; the things he said and the names he called people. They are going to come to you and say, 'Daddy, why did you do those things back then?' What I want to know, Mr. Carville, is: What are you going to tell those girls?"

That is a difficult but, one would have to say, a fair question. I would respond that I will tell my girls this: "There was a time in your Daddy's life when he had a good friend. And that good friend did a bad thing. And your Daddy did everything he could to try to forgive the bad thing and remember that this was a good friend. There will be times in your life when you are going to have good friends that do bad things. If you can, your father would like you to try to forgive the bad thing and stick with the good friend.

"But the most important lesson that I want you girls to take from all of this is that your father knows that you are good girls. And your father knows that sometimes in life even good girls do bad things. If that ever happens to you, the thing I want you to remember the most is that you come tell your Daddy about it. You know for sure that he'll stick with you."

# Sticking Together

**The title of this** book is *Stickin'*. It's primarily about sticking with the things you believe in: sticking with your family; your friends; your favorite sports teams; your political philosophy; your country; your God. Oftentimes in life, a powerful motivating factor in sticking with someone or something is the fact that people you dislike are trying to stick it to people you do like. In these cases, people know where they stand because they don't like the other side. This helps groups of people stick together when they might divide: The dislike of the other side can be a powerful adhesive.

This kind of sticking involves sticking it to your enemies. People are driven to act in a loyal manner by their hatred of the other side. This is a very human feeling—the enemy of my enemy is my friend. It's just human nature.

Take the Marquis de Lafayette, who fought for America in the Revolution. There are statues of him all over America. There's a wonderful city in Louisiana named after him. But make no mistake about it, Lafayette was not a loyal American. He was not an American hero. He was a French hero. He did fine things for America, but his first motivation was that he hated the British and was determined to get revenge on them.[1]

Nowhere have I encountered this phenomenon more obviously than during the Monica Lewinsky brouhaha. As I said in the last chapter, I did not have a very difficult time arriving at the decision to stick with the president. He had been awfully good to me. It was a case of a grown man acting stupid with a young woman. And I know that if I'd done anything that stupid, I'd have lied about it too.

But not everybody had the same view as me. Some people were very disturbed. They were genuinely upset and took a different line: They didn't think it was just about sex. I always felt I was defending a person. A person first, a principle second. They said their loyalty was to the Constitution or to the office rather than to the man. A lot of people believed their loyalty was higher than simply to a person. Some of these individuals felt burned by the president and they didn't feel particularly loyal to him. I didn't see it that way, but as I knew even then, loyalty is a complicated thing.

Ken Starr's $50 million inquisition and the intense media scrutiny were putting a lot of pressure on people. There was a worry among the rest of us that they might go public with their view of what the president did. Obviously this would have been a big step. It would have driven a big hole through the administration. But it wasn't something that anyone was going to do lightly.

One of the major problems for these people who felt something other than loyalty to Bill Clinton was the Republican party.

By going public against the president, they would in essence be helping people that they disliked on the other side. They would also be helping to advance the Republican agenda. These were the people we had all worked against and argued with and fought for years. The people we'd beaten to get into office in the first place. If you disagree with someone 20 percent of the time, and agree with them 80 percent of the time, why do you want to turn against them and help someone you disagree with 100 percent of the time?

I think this reluctance made a huge contribution to our cause. What kept people from crossing over was that they did not want to be on the other side. They were kept back by the opposition and who the opposition was and how they conducted themselves. I can't sit here and tell you what everybody was thinking but I know that it was a factor in a lot of people's minds. No matter what their doubts, the glue was stronger than the forces working against it. We stuck together behind the president.

As I said, there were other factors involved in people's decisions: People had a lot of reasons to stick with the president and some very positive feelings of loyalty. But this is a great example of a loyalty driven by dislike or even hatred of people in the opposition. As the Republicans became more inflexible and more shrill in their attacks on the president, the lines just got more and more partisan. This was to my glee, I might add. I was trying to do everything I could to make it as partisan as possible. And the more partisan the Republicans got, the more Democrats would come over to our side. Not only were people not going over to the other side, they were sticking. One of the cornerstones of my strategy was to incite Republicans. I knew that this would drive reluctant Democrats back to the president.

It's worth reminding ourselves what we were up against here. President Clinton is the most investigated president in history. He might be the most investigated person in history, I don't know. Investigations the likes of which no one has ever seen were unleashed on Bill Clinton. Lined up against the president was a seemingly unending array of prosecutors, investigators, probes, panels, and committees. The GOP Congress had no fewer than thirty-one inquiries into the Clinton administration.

We knew the Republicans were against us, but many of us suspected that the opposition to the president was very broadly based in what is described as the Washington Establishment. It didn't take a genius to figure out that a lot of the Establishment hated Clinton, but how much, we didn't know. We didn't know the full magnitude of the political opposition to the president.

Well, we got our answer. This was, for me, a vital moment in the whole affair. It came in the form of an excellent story on the Washington Establishment in the *Washington Post* written by Sally Quinn. The article was called "Not in Their Backyard" and it ran the day before the congressional elections, November 2, 1998, an election which would influence the impeachment vote.[2] Sally Quinn wrote that the Establishment is:

*Beltway insiders—the high-level members of Congress, policymakers, lawyers, military brass, diplomats, and journalists who have a proprietary interest in Washington and identify with it. They call the capital city their "town."*

The story went on to explain the attitude of these people toward Bill Clinton. Sally Quinn says she spoke to more than one hundred "Washingtonians" and clearly they were lining up to savage the president. It was incredible. The Establishment was sticking together and sticking it to the guy in the White House. The president, in the words of supposedly objective *Washington Post* columnist David Broder, "came in here and he trashed the place, and it's not his place." Poor little D.C. According to Muffie Cabot, who had been the Reagans' social secretary: "This is a demoralized little village." It is a village full of people called Muffie and Tish with a terribly strong sense of community. "We have our own set of village rules," said David Gergen of *U.S. News & World Report*.

So it's a village, a community, but it's a community that doesn't bear much resemblance to any in the rest of the country, whatever they might say. Trying to explain the difference between the Establishment and the rest of America, historian Michael Beschloss said, "When everything is turned upside down it affects our psyche more than someone who might be farming in Wyoming." Actually, Mike, Wyoming is more of a ranching state than a farming state. To someone who is ranching in Wyoming, a man having sex in Washington probably is a little less traumatic than what he has to deal with. Like his cattle getting brucellosis or something. A drought or a devastating livestock disease may well be a tad more upsetting than an act of consensual sex. But then again, Mike, that farmer is not from your village.

Now on the other hand, when it came time to talk about

Ken Starr, the cigarette lawyer, here was a man in extremely good standing with the Establishment. As Sally Quinn wrote:

*Ken Starr is not seen by many Washington insiders as an out-of-control prudish crusader. He has lived and worked here for years. He has a reputation as a fair and honest judge. He has many friends in both parties. Their wives are friendly with one another and their children go to the same schools.*

Ken Starr was one of their own.

Now, when those people who were wondering whether or not to stick with the president looked over to the other side, there was a different view. They saw not only Tom DeLay and Bob Barr (that should be enough to rally anybody), but also all the lawyers and the lobbyists and all the people that think they know more than anybody else.

Where would you go? They called the city their town as if they paid for the place, as if they own it. Who wants to be with them? And so our cause became a jihad. I got calls from people who said they had a problem with what the president had done, but seeing all these assholes who are against him, the hell with it! This was the icing on the cake.

Now, it's important to place this article in its correct context. About a week before it appeared, I was at a party for Sally Quinn and Ben Bradlee for their twentieth wedding anniversary filled with family, friends, and, of course, some of these Washington insiders. Ben Bradlee is a stand-up guy and is appropriately revered in Washington. People who have worked with Ben Bradlee hold him in immense affection and are very loyal to him. Some of them literally worship him. I don't know if I have ever run across someone who is as highly thought of as Ben Bradlee. Sally Quinn is also someone I know and like enormously. I have always gotten along with the two of them. Anyway, by the time of their party, it was apparent that the president was not going to be run out of office. Not only that, but he had not lost his effectiveness.

That morning or the morning before, the Wye River agreements had been signed. The president had played a huge part in keeping the Israelis and Palestinians at the table talking to each other. Netanyahu and Arafat both praised him. And King Hussein, who was a tremendously respected man in Washington, said he had known American presidents since Eisenhower but never one with Bill Clinton's "dedication, clearheadedness, focus and determination."[3]

That night, as I looked around, I suspected that all the people at the party hated the president. I also thought a substantial number were actually disappointed that he got the Wye agreement through because they couldn't use their argument that he'd lost his effectiveness. These people had tried to derail him by encouraging the biggest political witch-hunt ever and then trying to say his real problem was his ineffectiveness. It's like shooting someone and saying his real problem is he's bleeding. So I had a pretty good time, to say the least. I enjoyed myself. In a room full of people that I thought all hated the president.

And, lo and behold, a week later, the day before the election, the article by none other than my friend Sally Quinn herself appeared and it said explicitly what I had thought. It was all there in black and white in the *Washington Post*. Now it wasn't just anybody writing this, it was Sally Quinn. She's covered Washington a long time and she is more insightful on the subject than anyone. Sally knows all of these people and they were willing to talk to her and say what they were really thinking. There's an old saying that even a broken clock is right twice a day. I thought at least I was right this one time—the Establishment really did hate the president.

Now, some people in the administration got mad at Sally for writing this article, but there's a little bit of shooting the messenger there. Sally wrote a great news story and did a fine service. It was a fine piece of journalism. I know the president read every word of it. Very seldom do I disclose a conversation with the president, but I can say that I talked to him about this story. I distinctly remember it. I was giving a speech to a group of cardiologists and staying at the Mansion at Turtle Creek in Dallas. We had an amusing fifteen-minute conversation about the story and got a big kick out of the fact that it confirmed everything we suspected to be the truth.

The piece was liberating and almost fun. It gave us a real burst of energy. That was a great couple of days for me. The other great thing that happened, of course, was the day after the piece ran, we had the elections and the Democrats did better than anyone ever thought we could, showing how far out of touch the Establishment really was.

Now individually, I like a lot of the people Sally talked to.

But what rational person would want to be on the side of "Beltway insiders"? It is possible to loathe a group and like some of the people in it—people hate Congress but like their congressman. They think the public schools are terrible but they like the one their child's at. It's worth looking at this closely. We'll look at the opposition that was arrayed against the president in Washington as revealed in its full glory by Sally Quinn.

The members of the Washington Establishment are like educated wealthy people anywhere. They're nice, friendly, witty, charming. They're well mannered. They're well bred, whatever that means. They have nice homes. They have impeccable taste. The china matches the wallpaper. But they are different and they view themselves as different, as part of the elite. They had acquired many things, but the one thing that they had but were losing was their influence on and hold over the American people. More than bone china or Savile Row suits, the thing they wanted most was to be paid attention to.

They were frustrated and furious. They still are. More than being mad at Clinton, they're mad at this demise of their own influence. They're mad that for once they couldn't bully the American people. In the past, every time that the Establishment has told someone to go, to resign—in the end, they went. Nixon went, Gary Hart went, Joe Biden went. But not Bill Clinton.

Clinton survived the Gennifer Flowers thing and he got elected. And then Whitewater came along and they got their own guy Ken Starr in. And then what? Nothing. Zip. Nada. Whitewater produced nothing. Burned again. Then, Lewinsky

Who are the more thin-skinned: lawyers or journalists? Steven Brill is the editor-in-chief of *Brill's Content* magazine. He called me one time about a story he was working on about Kosovo. Before *Brill's Content,* he had worked on a magazine covering lawyers, and now he was doing one covering journalists. I asked Mr. Brill what the difference was between covering lawyers and journalists and he said the journalists are much more likely to want to sue you than the lawyers.

came. This was going to be the vindication. So they spent $50 million, and at the bottom of it all, what did they find? A grown man acting stupid with a young woman.

They were wrong again and again and again. And like a bad gambler, they just kept doubling their bet. They were sure that the public would come around to see what they knew from the beginning. But the president's approval ratings kept going up. In *The Death of Outrage,* Bill Bennett notes disapprovingly that the president's approval ratings reached 79 percent.[4] It's tough to get higher ratings than that. And the Establishment kept going at him. They were disconnected, out of it. They couldn't believe that the general population was not as sanctimonious as they and they blamed the American people. They lost and they got mad and told Sally Quinn about how the president was still around trashing "their 'town.'"

It was this whining that was so counterproductive. I mean, who wants to be aligned with these people? If they want their town, they should run the PTA and referee midget football. It might be their town, but it sure as hell ain't their country. Despite the fact that Bill Clinton was the twice-elected president of the United States, these people operated on their own agenda. They're not disloyal people, but rather than being loyal to the wishes of the people (i.e., you), they were and are loyal to themselves (i.e., not you). It's undemocratic. They think they know better than the hardworking men and women in the fifty states of this union, the people that voted for President Clinton.

Let me say this, the country will owe many debts of gratitude to Bill Clinton: for balancing the budget; leading a booming economy after inheriting an economic disaster; making significant progress in peace around the world from Northern Ireland to the Middle East; Kosovo; expanding family and medical leave. But the Establishment doesn't seem to be concerned with things like that.

It's clear that the Clintons themselves never were part of the Establishment. They'd never held any office in the city and their administration wasn't stuffed full of insiders. In an earlier article, Sally Quinn said, "They are viewed as having some sort of alien status, as being outsiders."[5] Part of this is because the Clintons are regular people. The president likes to jog and he goes to McDonald's. It was the same with Jimmy Carter. He was once attacked for carrying his own suitcase. The Establishment thought it was very undignified.

So what did the Establishment do when it wanted to attack the outsiders? It picked an insider for the job: Ken Starr. I have written a whole book on that subject and I recommend it to you.[6] That's all covered. I don't need to go back there.

Now, back in 1998, it would have been very easy for anyone to go over to the other side. Anyone could run to Ken Starr or some talk show with a negative story about the president. I was sticking already, but if the price of admission to that Establishment is stabbing someone in the back, I don't want that ticket. I'm too far out of the Beltway.

By and large, I just have a different worldview from the members of the Establishment. I didn't go to their schools, I don't talk their language. Some of their views are perfectly fine with me, but I wasn't going to change my behavior to please them. I think I'm old enough to be me. And anyway, I'm not interested in a career in politics in Washington and I shoot my mouth off way too much. I'm more than likely to say something I shouldn't and piss off someone important. The Establishment doesn't like loose cannons.

So where do all these people in the Establishment owe their loyalty? I think the Establishment is loyal to the Establishment. Enter an outsider who is also an energetic and progressive force of change like President Clinton and they perceive a challenge. They closed ranks and attacked. And when the president's people saw them in their true colors, we rallied and stuck together and defended him.

So there's something else the American people will owe Bill Clinton a debt of gratitude for. Even though it is not a fight he sought, he is the first person in history to take on the Washington Establishment and defeat it. In the future, maybe the

**There's another** tremendous disconnection in the way Washington looks at things compared to the rest of the country. In Washington, if you create a disaster and are able to walk away from it unscathed, you're thought to be shrewd. By any stretch of the imagination, the decision to grant clemency to the members of the FALN was viewed as a political disaster. You would have thought this whole thing ended up on the president's desk via an Immaculate Conception. That no one touched this. Well, it's not like Bill Clinton one day just got up and said: "You know, I think I'm going to grant clemency to these people from Puerto Rico."

Shortly after the whole thing came up, guess who went out on the Sunday talk shows by himself: yours truly. And the people from the prestigious law firms with their Ivy League degrees: You couldn't find a one of them—every one of them was in the tall grass. These are the same kinds of people that clink cocktail glasses with the crowd in Washington and talk about "these despicable political consultants with their thirty-second ads, their lack of principles, their mercenary view of the world." These are the kinds of people that use words like "governance" and "integrity" and that kind of bullshit that means nothing but hot air.

I guess a sign of getting old is that things that used to make you mad now make you laugh. I used to find these people contemptible, but really it's just funny and to some extent pathetic that they go and create a situation and let some C student from LSU go out and deal with it. "We don't want to soil our Stanford

Law degree or our Harvard MBA. We don't want to look bad at the club or at the partners' meeting at the law firm. It could be bad on our résumé in case we want to be deputy secretary of state for interglobal development someday." If you had created a political disaster of this magnitude you would probably want to get out and fight back, but not them. They want to hide. It's just another precise example of when people look at Washington and they say, "Gee these people are different from me." The reason is, they *are* different from you.

people who run Washington will think more like the people in the rest of the country (all of you good people out there). The people have sent a clear message to the people in Washington and the Washington Establishment: We don't think like you.

This was the feeling that was really galvanized by the reaction to Sally Quinn's article. With the party lines drawn in Congress and the terrible behavior of the president's opponents only getting worse, our sense of solidarity behind Bill Clinton was strengthened. We all understood exactly what we were up against and we became determined to stick together.

I do think this all helps to prove a valuable lesson about loyalty. The lesson is that loyalty can be stimulated by your enemies, by the people who don't think like you or are against you or hate you. I don't think that it's a bad thing, it's just the way we are. If you pull for a team, you often have a historic rival. I'm a big LSU fan and Ole Miss is our historic rival, so I'm glad when Ole Miss loses when they play someone else.

## The *Post* and Ken Starr

If you want to draw a diagram of the Washington Establishment you could draw a triangle like the one they use for food groups. At the top of the triangle, where the fatty stuff is, would be the Washington Post Company: *Newsweek* and the *Washington Post* most prominently.

The *Post* is an important component of the Establishment, and it is very loyal to it. And the *Post* has also been loyal to that other Establishment figure, Ken Starr. We talked about leaks in the last book. There were leaks all over the place. A lot of them went to *Post* reporter Susan Schmidt, whom Steven Brill described as doing "stenography for the prosecutors."[7] The *Post* editorial page was very loyal to Ken Starr too.

Now, to my knowledge, during the Clinton presidency the editorial page has never acknowledged a certain connection between Ken Starr and the *Washington Post*.

The connection goes back to 1987, when there was a landmark libel decision. Mobil Oil CEO William P. Tavoulareas and his son sued the *Post* over a 1979 report that Tavoulareas had "set up" his son in a company that did business with Mobil. The paper lost and a jury awarded Tavoulareas $2 million. A three-judge appeals court upheld the verdict, but the full Court of Appeals reversed the decision. The judge who co-wrote the opinion was . . . Ken Starr.[8] And as I said, I can't find where the *Post* has mentioned that, and with all due respect, they should have.

It's actually not that easy to find any mention of the Starr-

*Post* connection other than in passing in bios of Starr. Todd Gitlin talked about it in the *Washington Monthly.*[9] Mollie Dickenson wrote about it in *Salon* magazine on the Internet.[10] But I cannot see that it has been mentioned in the *Post* during the whole period when Ken Starr was the *Post*'s hero.

Now here's the $2 million question: Should they have mentioned that Ken Starr let them off the hook for all that money? I think so. I was a lawyer, I remember how it goes. You lose in trial court, you're upset; you lose in appeals court, you're more upset; you come back and a judge offers an opinion that lets you off the hook, well, he's your hero. You naturally are going to have a sense of loyalty to that person. I would almost side with the *Post* on this one. Heck, if somebody let me off the hook for a couple of mil', I'd probably stick with them too. (But then again, is sucking up to Ken Starr worth $2 million? Give me a week and I'll get back to you on that one.)

So sticking may not always come just from the best of motives. We're human beings. We love our friends, we loathe our enemies. There is a combination of factors pulling you toward your friends and pushing you away from your enemies. I can't say what the combination was in this case, but I know it was operating, helping our side stick together.

**Another example** of how disconnected the Washington Establishment is from the rest of the world can be found in a couple of NBC/*Wall Street Journal* polls. Of all the polls, this one carries the most weight among political professionals. It is conducted by my friend Peter Hart, one of the best-known Democratic pollsters of the last twenty years, and Bob Teeter, a hell of a classy guy and a renowned Republican pollster. Both men are properly honored and respected for their knowledge and integrity.

There was an NBC/*Wall Street Journal* poll conducted on President Clinton's approval ratings in July 1998, before the president testified. The results were that his personal favorable rating was 50 percent, and his job favorable rating was 63 percent.

After one year of pontificating and howling, of the Establishment going on TV and writing editorials and Op-Ed columns, of cable TV jocks spouting their nauseating stream of vindictiveness, of the horror and the shock, of the village being tizzified about an act of consensual sex going on in their midst, one year later, there was another poll. President Clinton's personal favorable rating was 50 percent and his job favorable rating was 62 percent. So if you really want to know the power of the Washington Establishment, this is it: They can cost you one point on your job rating.[11]

## Postscript

I've got to mention this report, which can serve as a postscript to this section and to my last book. Ken Starr turns out to have been a sore loser. At a public meeting in Los Angeles in September 1999, Ken Starr said that he should have left the Office of the Independent Counsel after Whitewater. Someone else should have taken over. "In retrospect I made a serious mistake." Not only that, but he said he never liked the independent counsel law, which expired in June 1999. "The statute simply does not work." Now if he'd listened to old Uncle James back in 1994 and quit, he would have saved himself all this trouble and he wouldn't be feeling so sorry for himself now.

# Sticking It to My Enemies

**When I was out** there on these talk shows, defending the president, people would say, "If a Republican had done that, you would be attacking them and not defending them." Well, of course I would. I am not a loyal Republican. I am not an objective person. I have a point of view. I have friends, and yes, I am going to cut a friend or a person I agree with some slack. The idea that people in Washington think there is something wrong with this, well, I don't know if it amuses me or annoys me. But what an idiotic question! Why would I give the same degree of loyalty, the same degree of forgiveness, the same degree of passion to Bob Barr that I would to Teddy Kennedy? I told you these people were different.

I'd say to those people asking the question: I'm not a hypocrite, you just don't get it. A friend and someone that you agree with will get a better break than a jerk. I'm not likely to say, "That Bob Barr is a fine man. I should listen to what he has to say." As we've seen, the opposition to the president was heavy with jerks like this. Many of them became good old-fashioned enemies. As I said in the previous chapter, there were reasons why people couldn't go over to the other side. And many of the reasons were personified in these enemies of the president in the Congress of the United States.

But just what constitutes an enemy? I guess you know one when you see one. Certainly the president's congressional enemies were easy to spot. And in Luke 11:23, we read, "He that is not with me is against me." In electoral politics there's a way of measuring whether people are for you or against you and that's whether they vote for you or your guy. It's our job to persuade people that it is in their best interest to vote for our side. I usually assume that someone will be with me until they demonstrate that they aren't. So the way I look at it, all voters are potential Democrats. Everyone I meet might turn out to be a friend.

A loyal person is one who sticks with their friends. If you have a friend and your friend is being attacked by someone, that someone becomes your enemy too. That's part of sticking with your friends. I mean, in the course of your daily life, if you are a combative kind of person, you pick up enemies along the way. In politics, everyone takes sides, so it's the nature of the work to make a lot of professional enemies. Some of these become personal enemies too.

Machiavelli had something to say about enemies. In Chapter 21 of *The Prince*, he says, "A prince is also respected when he is a true friend and a true enemy; that is, when he declares himself on the side of one prince against another without reservation."[1] What he means is: Don't sit on the fence. If you see two of your neighbors getting into it, he says, you better declare an interest in one of them because they'll both resent it if you

## Carville's Twelve Rules of Sticking It to Your Political Enemies

1. **Attack:** Make sure you go on the offensive right away. Rush the passer. Blitz. Send the linebackers, send the cornerbacks. Send the punter in from the sidelines. I said this in the *Wall Street Journal* in 1990 and I've stuck with it: "It's hard for somebody to hit you when you've got your fist in their face." This is especially noteworthy when you are up against it. When your defenses are crumbling, the best thing to do is go on the offense.

2. **Respond:** If they attack you, make sure you respond.

3. **Get the facts:** Do the research, do the polling. There's nothing worse than getting screwed on a fact.

4. **Don't get surprised:** If there is something worse than getting screwed on a fact, it's being surprised.

5. **Keep it partisan:** In a fight, the opposition *always* sucks at *everything*.

6. **Go with your gut:** The head has never beaten the gut in a political argument yet.

7. **Be tough:** It's not a game. There is always a lot at stake for the candidate and for the country. As far as you're concerned, the race is everything, so there's no point holding back.

8. **Be intense:** This is a variation on number seven. If you're on *Larry King* with someone from the other side, don't get too chummy. Interrupt; beat them back; ask Larry to let

you finish. Don't let the other guy finish. Stay on your game. The other guy should be sweating bullets he's trying so hard to keep up.

9. **Worry about timing:** Don't get too far out there with your attacks on your own if you're just the adviser. You often need to wait. Once the press attacks the other guy, for example, it's safe to pile on.

10. **Attack when the other guy isn't expecting it:** Every military strategist knows the value of surprise. You should too.

11. **Stick it from a distance:** Try to avoid meeting people you're sticking it to because you might find you like them. (No one ever said that about Ken Starr: "If you only knew Ken . . ." They actually did say that about David Sentelle, who was the presiding judge of the panel that appointed Ken Starr.)

12. **Get revenge:** Remember:

Hatred is by far the longest pleasure:
Men love in haste, but they detest at leisure.
—Lord Byron, *Don Juan*

don't help. And if you join in and pick the winner, he'll owe you one; and the loser will at least remember you when he's back on the upside. What worked for Machiavelli in the early 1500s might not fly today, but it's something to bear in mind.

Certainly, if there's a fight between a bunch of Democrats

**I just** love it when big corporations get involved in politics and try to be cute. During the last World Series, Pizza Hut began running an ad on TV that showed a Hillary Clinton look-alike (who looks about as much like Mrs. Clinton as I do) eating pizza at what looks like a campaign rally. She praises the pie, saying she knows so much about New York pizza "'cause, New York, I wanna be your next senator." A cop character then says of the "un-New York" price of the pizza, "What do they think this is? Arkansas?"

Now, why do we care about this? Well, New York City mayor and Senate hopeful Rudolph Giuliani has been going on and on about the less-than-extraordinary fact that Mrs. Clinton (who might run for the Senate from New York) has had the audacity to live and work outside the confines of the Empire State, including time in Arkansas. So the ad looks like it's knocking Mrs. Clinton on Giuliani's terms.

Now, it turns out that Pizza Hut's parent is something called Tricon Global Restaurants. And Tricon has recently contributed $2,500 to Giuliani. And Tricon board member Kenneth Langone happens to be co-chair of Giuliani's Senate fund-raising campaign, which helped raise $136,000 for Giuliani's 1997 mayoral campaign. And when Pizza Hut launched a New York–themed pizza in 1999, they did it with a City Hall press conference. As Clinton aide Howard Wolfson said, "Quite a set of coincidences."[2]

They want to get involved in politics? Here's some politics. As soon as I saw this, I wanted to say that no good Democrat should have anything to do with Pizza Hut. This is not a coincidence. I said it when I heard about the ad in October and I'm saying it now: Just don't buy the stuff.

After all, this ain't too much of a sacrifice. It's always been impossible to distinguish between Pizza Hut pizza and the box it comes in. Loyal Democrats: Don't go in the restaurants either. Again, the hardship is small. Asking someone not to eat at Pizza Hut is like asking them to give up Brussels sprouts for Lent.

and a bunch of Republicans, I know that I'm not going to sit on the fence.

As we know, we've seen the worst kinds of attacks, the most vicious partisan garbage dumps, from Republicans in the last few years. Many of the people involved in the attacks were not operating either from firm ground or with a full deck. The most prominent feature of the attacks was the breathtaking amount of hypocrisy involved.

I always feel duty-bound to point out Republican hypocrisies. I wouldn't be a loyal Democrat if I didn't. These blatant hypocrisies also help to cast some light on what some Republicans really think about certain things like family values, loyalty to the institution of marriage, and sticking with one's spouse. We'll see in the next chapter that there have been some remarkable examples of hypocrisy in this area. Breathtaking.

My experience has been that the people who talk the loudest about morality are the people who possess the least amount of it. Those who talk about family values—watch them peel off from their wives and leave their children at home. Republicans love to talk about the family. They will go on and on about the sanctity of the family and good Christian values and how these are threatened by one-parent families, gay people, and Democratic policies. And Republican congressmen really believe in the institution of marriage. They're all for it. I guess that's why they get married so many times. My problem with the Republican obsession with family values is that they will criticize everybody in the world but themselves.

Am I mad about Newt Gingrich talking about the destruction of values and leaving his wife for a so-called choirgirl? Well, no, because to get mad at Republican hypocrisy is the same as getting mad at the air. It's just there, what can you do about it?

Now, once we have identified our enemies, there are a couple of things we can do: stay out of their way or get in their face. If you've read Carville's Twelve Rules elsewhere in this chapter you'll see that there's not a lot of talk about avoiding your enemies. So you go get 'em. There's no sitting on the fence.

I can recall the precise moment when I decided to really step up the battle against Ken Starr. We'll see in the course of our look at loyalty that a lot comes down to instinct rather than planning or design, and this was one of those occasions.

When the Lewinsky story broke in January 1998, Mary and I were on a West Coast trip. We'd gone up to San Francisco, where we have part ownership in a restaurant,* to have dinner.

---

*Hawthorne Lane. For reservations call 415-777-9779. It's excellent. Tell them James sent you.

## Lott, Barr, and the CCC

I might be pushing at an open door here, but I want to say something about the odious Council of Conservative Citizens and the Republicans who have been associated with it. Alan Dershowitz said that Bob Barr had spoken at a CCC convention in Charleston, South Carolina, in June 1998 and Trent Lott's links have been even closer. There's been some good reporting in, among other places, the *Washington Post,* the *New York Times,* and *Salon* magazine on the Internet.

Make no mistake about it, the CCC is a racist organization. If you look at its Web site, you can read about Abraham Lincoln, the tyrant, "the most evil American in history," who deprived Southerners of their "way of life" (we know what that means). And you can read some truly disgusting abuse of Martin Luther King. In the *New York Times,* Bob Herbert quoted the Southern Poverty Law Center as saying the CCC is "the reincarnation of the racist White Citizens Councils of the 1950's and 1960's." They describe its *Citizens Informer* publication as a "steady stream of anti-black and anti-homosexual columns." Colbert King wrote in the *Post* that Trent Lott spoke to the CCC in 1992 and was pictured on the front of the *Citizens Informer* publication in 1997. Thomas Edsall wrote in the *Post* about Lott being a columnist for it. Lott claimed not to know about the CCC's views. To have "no firsthand knowledge of the group's views." No awareness at all. As Bob Herbert said: "Spare me."[3]

The story was everywhere; there was no getting away from it. It was a Saturday. I had done Larry King's show a little earlier and I was due to do *Meet the Press* for Tim Russert the next day, January 25. It would have been unseemly to disappear at that point, tempting as that might have been.

That Saturday night at dinner, I probably got into the wine a little heavier than I should have. The next morning, I was up pretty early to tape the show in the hotel where we were staying. We had to prepare the show for an early East Coast transmission. It was around six o'clock in the morning and I was coming down in the elevator. At that point, I have to admit that I really didn't have a good idea of what I was going to say on the program.

Well, instinctively I suppose, I said to myself that the best defense really is a good offense. I decided that now would be the time to declare war on Ken Starr. I could see where this whole thing was going. I knew this was a fight for the long haul and I knew which side I was going to be on. As the Brits would say, in for a penny, in for a pound.

You don't get a chance to win all the wars you fight but I'm sure glad we won this one. I was pleased to see a clip from that appearance. A segment of it was rerun on *Meet the Press* at the end of October 1999, just after Ken Starr resigned. Starr was on the show and we saw a reprise of yours truly stickin' it for the first time. I really was looking a bit ragged, trying hard not to say something I shouldn't.

When I declared war that day in January 1998, I was hungover. I'd been undecided about what to say, partly because my head was a bit like a regular morning in San Francisco—rather foggy. The decision was made somewhere between the ninth floor and the lobby of the hotel. I think this was a real case of instinct taking over. I went with my gut and started to stick it to my enemies right then and there.

# Drawing
# the Line

**I've explained why I** stuck with Bill Clinton and some of the things that made us stick together on our side. Now I want to try to answer another question that people put to me. "Okay," they said, "you're sticking. But what would make you leave? Under what circumstances would you abandon your guy? Where do you draw the line?" I am generally skeptical of people who try to say what they would do in hypothetical situations. But let me take a stab at what would get me to say, "I am out of here."

We can give the benefit of the doubt—there are people who are genuinely offended by sexual misconduct. They are not just pretending to be horrified by it. Furthermore, if we extend the benefit of the doubt, there are people who are offended that someone would try to cover it up and not admit it. Well, I've said that I would cut a friend a break when they have done a bad thing, and in my book, you don't abandon a guy over sex. To me, that particular bad thing is this side of the line. I have had some genuine disagreements with people over this.

So people say, "James Carville: You don't draw the line at sex, you don't even draw the line at lying about sex. Where do you draw the line? Do you even have one?" Well there is a line, of course. I want to set out some things that decidedly cross the line as far as James Carville is concerned. In my world, the most egregious thing that a person can do is not to take care of his family and his kids. It's easy for me to stay on that side of the line as far as sexual misconduct is concerned. Child neglect is a much bigger deal.

It's almost too easy, but we only need refer once more to the glorious career of Newt Gingrich. I'm not doing this to kick this guy around. I already kicked him around in *We're Right, They're Wrong*. I'm doing it because of the sheer hypocrisy we just mentioned. And even though Newt's gone, it's kind of hard to write a book without bringing him up.

Some background here. Even in 1974, as he ran for Congress, he developed a reputation in some circles as a "ladies' man."[1] Newt did not believe oral sex was sex. (A woman said of a tryst in 1977 that "we had oral sex. . . . Then he can say, 'I never slept with her.'"[2])

On election night in 1978, some of his staff were placing bets on how long his marriage would last. If you had eighteen months, you won the pool. In April 1980, he asked his wife, Jackie, for a divorce. Jackie had suffered from uterine cancer in 1978 and needed another operation to have another tumor removed when Newt decided he wanted a new wife. He thoughtfully decided to visit her in the hospital. In the words of

Lee Howell, who worked as Gingrich's press secretary for part of the 1970s:

*Newt came up there with his yellow legal pad, and he had a list of things on how the divorce was going to be handled. He wanted her to sign it. She was still recovering from surgery, still sort of out of it, and he comes in with a yellow sheet of paper, handwritten, and wants her to sign it.*[3]

So there's Newt trying to get his wife to sign divorce papers while she's lying on a hospital bed. Next, we have Newt's level of concern for his own family. His former campaign treasurer, L. H. "Kip" Carter, described the sorry scene in a *Frontline* documentary in 1996:

*Jackie and the kids were down there in that house with no food and, you know, electricity and water and all that sort of stuff. So at the First Baptist Church and some other places in town, we took up money and we took up canned food and took it down to the house so that she could keep the lights on and keep the kids fed.*[4]

(Six months after the divorce from Jackie, Newt married Marianne Ginther.)

Now if someone I was associated with had done all that, I'd say, "Man, I'm so out of here, you'll never find me. I don't want to remember that I even knew you." But this kind of behavior doesn't seem to bother Washington one bit.

This is, of course, the same Newt who initially accepted a $4.5 million book advance from Rupert Murdoch while Murdoch had an interest in legislation involving Fox that was before Congress.[5] And the Newt who'd relentlessly gone after then Democratic speaker Jim Wright in the late 1980s, partly over a book deal about one-seventieth the size of his. (Newt was reprimanded for the book deal by the House Ethics Committee, the same committee he used against Wright.) And the Newt the Federal Election Commission sued (with GOPAC, the Republican political action group Gingrich headed from 1986) over illegal use of funds[6] and whose former pastor the Reverend Brantley Harwell said, "I think Newt is amoral when it comes to politics."[7]

Now forget what I think for a second, but there's something glaringly obvious that needs saying at this point. We can see that while he was in power over there in Congress, Mr. Gingrich did not seem to have crossed any lines as far as the Republicans were concerned. It doesn't seem as though it's possible to go too far as long as you are in power or being useful to them. As long as the Republicans remain loyal to the power that you wield, you can get away with pretty much anything.

Let's ask Mr. Bill Bennett. He did, in his *Book of Virtues*, single out loyalty as a virtue, so he knows something about that. He is also fond of drawing lines and "speaking truth to power," as he put it in his book *The Death of Outrage*.[8] Well, his own outrage died somewhere along the way. If you want to point out the precise spot where Mr. Bennett's personal outrage reached a demise, you can. It's like finding the corpse of the last dodo.

Bill Bennett's outrage died as soon as it came face-to-face with its first Republican in a position of power.

Our "values czar" likes to say, "This he knew." Well, he knew all this stuff about Gingrich. But this was up-and-coming Newt and Speaker Newt. So what did Bennett say? Nothing. He was too ecstatic about the "Republican Revolution." He knew all this and he never said a word. It was fine. It's only when Newt's out of power that we hear anything. Gingrich loses his job when he listens to Bill Bennett's advice. He's out of power and then there's outrage about Newt leaving his second wife. There's no power there to be loyal to anymore.

And look at *The Death of Outrage* itself. Well, the only active Republican politician Bill Bennett criticizes by name in this book is Dan Quayle.[9] (How active he is after pulling out of the race for the Republican presidential nomination is open to question. If brain waves are a measurement of activity, he barely registers.) That's just not fair. We all know it's not nice to pick on people like Dan Quayle. Pick on someone your own size. I mean, wow! He really went after a political colossus there, a guy with real clout. The lesson here, cowboys and cowgirls at home, is if you're in power you're right. If you win, anything you do is all right with Bill Bennett. The sin is losing the power. So Bill Bennett is a loyal guy—he's loyal to two things: power and pork chops.

"Wait a minute," I hear someone say. "Here's James Carville criticizing someone for being partisan. That's a bit rich." Well I would say this: I haven't set myself up, or allowed myself to be set up, as a protector of the nation's morals. It's my job to be partisan. Bill Bennett's book is called *The Book of Virtues,* not *The Book of Republican Virtues,* a tome whose only feature would be its extreme brevity.

I got a little sidetracked there, but you get the point. There's a tremendous double standard operating here. And it's not confined by any means to Bill Bennett. It's a Republican trait. It's been the same with Pat Buchanan. When he was a Republican, he could do no wrong. He could speak at their forums and even at the Republican convention. He could run for president; he could do whatever he liked. No one ever brought up the things he had said. No one ever mentioned them when he was in a position to help them.

But the minute Pat Buchanan said he might join the Reform party and stand against the Republicans, then they said something. His sin was that he was now threatening to hurt them politically. All of a sudden, people recalled some of the things he'd said. "Did you know Pat thought this stuff?" they cried. "We're shocked." One of the main things people fixed on was some of the views about the Second World War that he put in his new book, *A Republic, Not an Empire.* Well, I would think they knew already that Pat Buchanan had some revisionist views about World War II. To quote *The New Republic,* "Buchanan's fixation with the not-so-bad side of Hitler (and the not-so-good side of President Roosevelt's opposition to him) is not just long-standing—it's practically lifelong."

The piece quotes a column in which Buchanan concedes that Hitler was genocidal, a racist, and an anti-Semite but that *[h]e was also an individual of great courage, a soldier's soldier in the Great War, a political organizer of the first rank, a leader steeped in the history of Europe, who possessed oratorical powers that could awe even those who despised him.*[10]

This column was written in 1977. ("Did you know Pat thought these things . . . ?") Now you want to talk about drawing the line. Deep down inside with every fiber of my body I believe that if someone spoke at our convention who had the views of Mr. Pat Buchanan, I'd just carry my coon ass right out of the building. I really don't think I could have sat there and watched it. I think I would have carried my ass out. And if you can't see the difference between all that and a sexual indiscretion, I can't explain it to you.

So long as these figures are in positions of power in the Republican party, no lines are drawn at all. Newt Gingrich never bothered anybody with what he did to his family until he lost his power. Pat Buchanan's views weren't a problem until he mentioned the Reform party. Gingrich and Buchanan's sin was that they weren't going to help these guys anymore. Suddenly, the scales fell from the Republicans' eyes. Hallelujah! They saw the light. Take away the power and the truth is kind of naked.

For Republicans, when there is a power outage, you get loss-of-power outrage. You can do anything you want when you're in power. The Republicans will remain loyal to the power, never mind the person who's wielding it. If you don't raise your kids right but you are for a capital gains tax cut, that's great. If

## The Stickin' Award

Bill Bennett shouldn't worry about the death of outrage—he's outraged enough for the rest of us. In 1995, he and his cohorts went after television talk shows after having scored a great victory for freedom by persuading Time Warner to sell off its interest in Interscope Records, home of acts like Dr. Dre, Snoop Doggy Dogg, Tupac, and Nine Inch Nails. Now, there's not much danger of upsetting anyone in a position of power in the Republican Establishment going after daytime talk shows and rock music. They're pretty easy targets. Bennett has continued to attack the specter of rock music. In an article in 1997, he went at it again, bemoaning a lack of corporate self-restraint at Seagram/Universal, Sony, BMG, "and others exploiting the youth rebellion instinct."[11]

In 1999, after the Littleton tragedy, the Czar appeared on *Meet the Press*. He went after a familiar cast: "The Levins, the Bronfmans, the people who run Viacom." In congressional testimony right after that he attacked "the Edgar Bronfmans, Howard Stringers, Michael Eisners, and Oliver Stones" (I'll have to ask my friends in Israel if they detect any pattern here. I'm sure I'm just being a little paranoid), i.e., the usual Time Warner, Universal, filmmaker, Hollywood class of guy and anyone, as Frank Rich pointed out, who was absolutely anyone in the entertainment industry and wasn't Rupert Murdoch.[12]

Well, by the time Frank Rich had gotten going, the wind must have changed. Because in September 1999, Bennett's media watchdog group, Empower America, finally mentioned Murdoch and gave him a "silver sewer" award, primarily for the show *Action*. You would have thought that Rupert Murdoch's network had put that show on completely out of character. Bill Bennett had no idea that this sainted man would put this kind of show on television just to make a dollar.

Let's see what he knew before Frank Rich attacked Murdoch. Fox has been the most controversial network for years. To protect his ass, he finally had to say something about the new show. There were about six "f's" bleeped out in the scenes before the opening credits. The one black guy was a pimp. There were Jewish jokes. I mean, come on. All of a sudden he's outraged? *Action* had almost no audience. The September 23 Nielsen ratings measured five million viewers; a 3.4 rating, a 5 share (that's 5 percent of the TVs in use), and a rank of ninety-fifth, and soon the show was on hiatus. So he wasn't exactly putting a lot on the line attacking that show. (Maybe they should rename the show *Cut*.) So, again, if you are out of power or low in the ratings, Pork Chop Bill will be glad to take a shot at you. And shooting this show was like shooting a dead person.

Back home we called people like Bill Bennett who were loyal to power "front-runners." When you were on top, they were right there. As soon as you had a reverse, they were gone. Bill Bennett likes giving out awards. Well, let's give him one. He gets the Stickin' Award for sticking with power. It's the first Suck Up to Power Award, and it will consist of a set of silver lips fixed to an ample posterior.

you are a good parent but you think people ought to pay their fair share, it's terrible. There's the death of outrage.

So I think I can answer the question I posed at the beginning of the chapter. How bad would something have to be to make me leave the president? Well, I know if he had tried to divorce Hillary, if he had tried to get a property settlement from her when she was recovering in the hospital from cancer surgery, and the church had to take Chelsea in, and he tried to take a $4.5 million advance from someone who had as much business before the government as anybody, I got to tell you, I would have left him. I would have said, "I don't care, I am checking out of here. Even I can't stand this." Which puts me in a decidedly different position from that of the Republicans.

We can ask again, how bad does the bad thing have to be? The bad thing lies somewhere between acting stupid with a young girl and not wanting people to find out about it and trying to divorce your wife on her sickbed. It lies between a sexual indiscretion and running out on your family and not taking care of your kids. Sex, no; running out on your family and not taking care of your kids, yes.

If you're asking, here is the line. I would attack a fellow Democrat if they did this. I ain't defending a son of a bitch who doesn't take care of his kids. Nor am I going to defend someone who says how Hitler had a point. So there's my answer, Mr. right-wing-pontificating-family-values-absolute-need-for-moral-parameters-disgust-with-people-having-sex-and-drinking-beer-and-scratching-their-ass-and-everything-else. You want your line, you've got your line.

# In Theory

**In the Introduction, I** said that I think people have a yearning for something to hold on to. They are looking for connections, and for a sense of loyalty in their lives; for people and principles to stick with. That is why we are making the case for loyalty. The difficult part is figuring out which people and which principles. It's difficult to sit down and make a list of the things a person is loyal to in theory. I do think you can say that along the road you need markers and guideposts: This is where you are, and this is the direction you need to go in. These are things you can be loyal to. But in practice it's more complicated. And events will always conspire to present people with dilemmas and choices that will test their loyalty.

You do have markers in life that help to define who you are. First you have your family, your foremost marker in your life; then your country, your religion, your friends, and on down the line. A lot of times, these choices are very simple—LSU plays Alabama, I'm for LSU. The right thinks all choices are that simple, but they're not. They're not all LSU or Alabama. They're much more difficult and they can change over time.

**For a** more academically based treatment of this subject, I would refer you to a work called *Loyalty* written in 1993 by a professor of law at Columbia, George P. Fletcher. He makes some very interesting and some very telling points about loyalty. His thesis, as best as I can tell, is that we have a "historical self" that relates to the circumstances in which we're born: the country we're born in, our culture, our religion. From that, certain loyalties derive. We have a genetic loyalty, a DNA. So an American can't just decide to declare loyalty to France because he likes the food. And for me: I was born in Louisiana, therefore I'm for LSU, and I'm for the USA, and the Roman Catholic Church.

He further divides loyalty into three categories: loyalty to people (based on love—your friends, your family, your spouse); group loyalty; and loyalty to God. Other kinds of loyalty, like lawyer-client relationships, are deviations from true loyalty because they're based on a contract. Fletcher goes on to an explanation of degrees of loyalty: The minimum we expect is "Thou shalt not betray me" (the least you can do is not take another lover); the maximum is "Thou shalt be one with me." There will be conflicts between the loyalties and about the degree, and everyone has to figure out a balance between the loyalties and having a separate moral judgment on something. He mentions Claus von Stauffenberg, who was a member of the bomb plot against Hitler in 1944 as a German patriot. He used his judgment to override a loyalty to Hitler.[1]

All in all, it's not a weekend-at-the-beach read, but he says some fascinating things. He took on a subject not a lot of other people have been willing to undertake. I hope that in a much simpler, visceral way, as opposed to his more complex, cerebral way, my book can add something to the way people look at loyalty and the complexities and difficulties that are associated with it.

As for the guideposts, there is a need for some definitive stances. There should be some lines in the sand. "This is a principle that I believe in, and I'm going to stick with it. I'm loyal to it." Murder is wrong. That's an easy one. But what about the death penalty? In the Bible you can find ideas that seem contradictory: an eye for an eye and turn the other cheek. So it ain't that clear.

I have my own internal conflicts about the death penalty. I didn't lose a wink of sleep over Ted Bundy. But in most cases, it's much more difficult. I waver between the two positions on the death penalty. I am either the most for the death penalty of anyone who is against the death penalty, or I am the most against the death penalty of anyone who is for the death penalty. I waver in that great 55–45 zone. Right now, I think it would be better if we didn't have it. Is it worth killing one innocent person? Given human imperfection, there is no guarantee that it's not going to happen. We all mess up, but we usually mess up on much smaller things.

Now some politicians have taken a stand against the death penalty and made it one of their lines in the sand. Mario Cuomo is one. Cuomo was an extremely principled politician. He was absolutely against the death penalty and he remained loyal to that principle. When he was governor of New York, the Republican state legislature would pass a death penalty statute every year and every year Cuomo would veto it. His predecessor, Hugh Carey, did the same. Everyone knew where Mario Cuomo stood on the death penalty. He took a stand on it and stuck with it. He is one of the people who are able to take a position and be absolutely unwavering on it.

Many of these supposedly easy choices that involve principles like this are complex. What if you ask, "My country right or wrong?" Well, I'd say my country—but not always. I would not be loyal to my country in absolutely every circumstance. I don't think anyone would say that if they really thought about it. So in application, the question becomes a lot more difficult. If asked about it in theory, you might be able to say, "It depends." And what about the issue of abortion? Abortion is one of the most vexing and complicated issues there is.

Bob Casey was, outside of my own family, one of the finest men I ever knew. We worked with him on his campaign for governor of Pennsylvania. He raised eight kids and was a real stand-up guy. I remember a discussion he had with Harris Wofford, a Pennsylvania senator we also worked with and another fine man. Casey had a very fixed view about abortion—he was against it. It was not anything born or bred out of political expediency. He was even against exceptions for rape and incest. Wofford looked at the matter differently. He came to a different conclusion—he was pro-choice.

Casey told me one time that there is something to be said for the unexamined life. In one sense I understood what he meant.

When Paul Begala and I started working for him (Begala is my partner, lifelong friend, and also a really fine human being), Begala asked Casey if his father was a churchgoing man and Casey said, "My father was faithful to all his obligations." Casey didn't wrestle with the abortion thing, because his views about it were fixed. His own obligations mapped out a lot of his principles for him. That Casey and Wofford were loyal to different principles doesn't change the fact that they were both great men.

It becomes even tougher when a principle runs up against a loyalty, or loyalties are divided. Take Robert E. Lee in the Civil War. At the war's outbreak, Lee had been a member of the U.S. army for thirty-two years and he supported the idea of the Union. Although he owned slaves, he was somewhat opposed to slavery. But he stuck with Virginia. His loyalty to the South was greater than to the country as a whole. The day he resigned from the army Lee wrote to his sister in Baltimore. She was for the Union.

*With all my devotion to the Union and the feeling of loyalty and duty of an American citizen, I have not been able to make up my mind to raise my hand against my relatives, my children, my home.*[2]

One of the most celebrated cases of divided loyalty was that of Sir Thomas More, the Lord Chancellor to Henry VIII who was executed in 1535. Sir Thomas's martyrdom is venerated by the Catholic Church: He was made a saint by Pius XI in 1935. If you read up a little on More, you can see that he had a lot of crises of divided loyalties in his life.[3] He could have been a priest, for example, but decided he wanted to marry. He is celebrated because he refused to submit to the will of Henry VIII, who wanted to overturn the authority of the Church in Rome. Henry essentially wanted to marry whoever he wanted and the Church's restrictions on that got in the way.

More sat in the Tower of London. He could have gotten out if he had sworn an oath to Henry and his Act of Supremacy, but he wouldn't. He was the king's most trusted servant, but he went to the scaffold rather than deny his conscience. A contemporary account has it that More said as he waited for his head to be removed that he died the king's good servant but God's first.[4]

Entire communities can be judged disloyal. At the outbreak of the Second World War, the U.S. government simply assumed that Japanese-Americans would have divided loyalties and would choose Japan and be disloyal to the United States. So they shut them up in internment camps in one of the worst mass abuses of human rights in our history.

As I said in the Introduction, divided loyalties are one complicating feature, as is being either too loyal or loyal to something immoral or evil. I think it's possible to possess any virtue in the extreme. Slavish loyalty is wrong. It's sycophancy. And clearly being loyal to someone like Charles Manson is wrong. There has to come a time when you abandon ship, but it's tough to provide any guidelines about when to do so.

During Watergate, Republican Senator Barry Goldwater led a delegation to tell Richard Nixon his situation was hopeless, and he was right, it was. Nixon's party had abandoned him. But decisions that involve divided loyalties are terribly difficult and heart-wrenching and they must come down to personal conscience.

Thankfully, most of the choices we face are not like these, nor are they ones that vexed the great philosophers, ethicists, or even politicians. People have spent a lifetime of study on loyalty, and the concept becomes more elusive the further you get into it. It's impossible to get a theory or a definition to fit all circumstances. Life is very complicated. One size does not fit all. As the French would say about some of these ideas, "That's all very well in practice, but how does it work in theory?"

Even if loyalty is difficult to define, we can make the case for it. We go back again to our markers where the presumption is loyalty—the presumption is that our family is right, our friends are right, our country is right, our God is right. I would say that to most people it's instinctual. This prism that they see things through is basic and clear. The burden of proof against this is on the enemy—which doesn't mean they can't attain the burden of proof. But if you have gotten out there and acted pretty much on your instinct, you will have established your position. And I would also say that usually we go with the person—not the theory or the high-flown moral concept, but the person.

As we shall see, the guy in the foxhole at the Battle of the Bulge was not thinking about the fight between democracy and fascism. Nor was the average soldier defending Stalingrad thinking about saving communism from fascism. I believe that it is in battle that we see the most profound displays of loyalty. That deserves an entire chapter. Right now, we should take a practical viewpoint. What do you do in your everyday life? What do you choose to be loyal to every day?

Race was a very significant marker where I grew up. I would say that in southern Louisiana in my formative years, about 75 percent of the conversations we had were about race. When I was a kid, I used to instinctively pull for the team that had the most blacks. Now, I don't even think about it. That is some sort of progress.

Back then, I had a friend, Cyril Vetter, whose daddy had a tavern. It was in a town called Donaldsonville on Railroad Avenue and it was a segregated bar—they all were at that time. They used to show fights on the TV in the bar there. If I recall correctly, Wednesday was Pabst Blue Ribbon night and Friday was Gillette night. The bar would be full on these occasions: people sitting back, drinking beer, and watching the fights.

The tavern had a black cook called Emily. She would walk out of the kitchen and all the guys would be there in the bar watching the fights. Very often the contest would be between a black guy and a white guy and Emily would be for the black guy and the patrons would all be for the white guy. So she would say, "Who's winning?" If the white guy was winning, the men in the bar would say, "Stay out here and watch the fight, Emily," while if the black guy was winning they'd say, "Go back in the kitchen, Emily." It wouldn't matter if the black guy was from Jamaica and the white guy was from the U.S. or if the black guy was from the U.S. and the white guy was from Britain. Racial affiliation overcame national pride at that time in the Deep South. It was an instinctive thing.

There were two huge heavyweight fights before the war that divided a lot of loyalties: the two bouts between Alabama's Joe Louis and Max Schmeling of Germany at Yankee Stadium. When Schmeling knocked Louis out in the first fight, in 1936, a lot of white Americans were relieved that a black man was set back in his quest to become heavyweight champion of the world, which was the most prestigious title in sports at that time. Americans sent Schmeling telegrams congratulating him. There was a wire report from Congress: "Cheers for Max Schmeling's startling knockdown of Joe Louis stopped transaction of important business in the Senate." The reporter noted that it was Southern senators making the noise.[5]

By the time of the rematch in 1938, when Louis was world champion, Nazi Germany was on the rise and there was a lot of talk about the fight between democracy and fascism. But I think a lot of white people had divided loyalties. I suspect that a significant number of American whites, some of whom would go on to give their lives in the fight against Germany, would have pulled for Schmeling to beat Louis. White American Bundists went to Louis's training camp and laughed at him when he sparred. And when Louis beat Schmeling (he knocked him out in the first round), black people came out on the streets and celebrated. Louis describes it himself:

*The people in Harlem went wild, throwing bottles, tin cans and cups from rooftops—they had to call the police to stop them. In Cleveland, they had to use tear gas to stop the rioting. Black people all over the country were out in the streets, celebrating for me.[6]*

79

**Close your** eyes for a minute and think of loyalty. What comes first to mind? If the image was a flag or your country or the Constitution, then you're in line with what the dictionary writers think. Here's what you get from a selection of dictionaries:

*Merriam-Webster's Collegiate Dictionary,* tenth edition
**Loyal** 1. Unswerving in allegiance; a) faithful in allegiance to one's lawful sovereign or government; b) faithful to a private person to whom fidelity is due; c) faithful to a cause, custom, institution, or product. 2. Showing loyalty.

*Random House Webster's College Dictionary,* second edition
**Loyal** 1. Faithful to one's sovereign, government or state. 2. Faithful to one's oaths or obligations. 3. Faithful to any person or thing conceived as deserving fidelity or characterized by or showing faithfulness.

For a lot of people, it had nothing to do with democracy against fascism either—it was a black guy against a white guy.

People would have you believe that choosing to stick with something is the choice of a hair shirt. You don't allow yourself that wiggle room and your options are more limited than they would be if you allowed for a change of mind. And a change of mind might involve being disloyal. So, some would say, because you choose to be loyal, you choose to limit your chances for success.

But it's very important to remember that the sacrifice can

*American Heritage College Dictionary,* third edition
**Loyal** 1. Steadfast in allegiance to one's homeland, government or sovereign. 2. Faithful to a person, an ideal, a custom, or a duty. 3. Of, relating to, or marked by loyalty.

*Encarta World English Dictionary*
**Loyal** 1. Faithful. Remaining faithful to a country, person, ruler, government or ideal. 2. Expressing loyalty. Expressing or relating to loyalty.

*Oxford Dictionary and Thesaurus*
**Loyal** 1. True or faithful (to duty, love or obligation). 2. Steadfast in allegiance; devoted to the legitimate sovereign or government of one's country.

bring good. It is not just the act of being loyal that is rewarding, it is the consequences of that act. The friendship is tested, it passes the test, and, as a result, it is deepened. You have a better friend. The family gets more close-knit. The guy from the local service store comes to fix your broken heater on a Saturday night. The test can be very difficult. But it reminds you of the sign on the New Jersey Turnpike: The inconvenience is temporary; the improvement is permanent. (We might ask, if it's so goddamned permanent, why do they need to redo it every five years?) Loyalty has to be tested, but the relationship is permanent.

Looked at from this perspective, we can see that loyalty is an investment. Every small act of loyalty—a supportive phone call or letter, a loan of money, or whatever builds up in a kind of loyalty bank that you can draw on later. It's not a cynical transaction because that's not why you do it, the payback is not why you are loyal. Obviously you can't assume that you'll get full value in return, and we can see that in many relationships there's one person who puts more into it than the other, but if you don't put in anything, you've got no reason to expect anything in return.

What are we left with? Complicated moral and ethical questions that can't, for most people, be easily reduced to simple answers. If you have to pin me down to ask me what to be loyal to, stick with your best instinct. The further I get into the question of loyalty, the more I am reminded of recess in seventh grade at St. Joseph's parochial school in Baton Rouge, Louisiana. As in most schoolyards, there'd be fights and rumbles between various groups of kids. When this was going on, you'd look out for your friends and they'd look out for you. For me, this is the essence of loyalty. It's recess in seventh grade and there's a pile-up and Stanley Civello is at the bottom of the pile. It's instinct and your instinct is to go in there and try to help him.

If you have to think about it, it may already be too late.

**Other than** George Fletcher's book, there's not a whole lot written about loyalty. One American philosopher gave a series of lectures to the Lowell Institute in Boston in which he said that the moral foundations of American society were being undermined and that we needed to look to loyalty to remake the country. This was in 1907! Josiah Royce made loyalty the core of a whole moral world.[7] He defined loyalty as "the willing and practical and thoroughgoing devotion of a person to a cause." It helps us find meaning in life because the cause is larger than just one person. Royce goes further to say that you must be loyal to loyalty. Any cause that furthers the general amount of loyalty in the world is good. To encourage this, Royce wants us to teach loyalty and train people in it. In the end, loyalty is the only thing that gives us a higher "unity of experience." And it's the only way to realize "spiritual triumph." This book was probably not a best-seller. I guess it could use some recipes and nowhere does Royce mention seventh grade recess.

There is another book that is mostly about economics called *Exit, Voice, and Loyalty* that is very dense. I guess I'm the one that's dense, but it does have some pertinent stuff (or so our in-house panel of Nobel laureates tells me). When a product or a service declines in quality, people either *exit* (quit) or they *voice* (complain). In business, exit drives out voice, while in other social groups, like families, tribes, churches, countries, you can't really exit. Loyalty makes people want to stay in an organization to try and change it. It stops people quitting. Just to show you how complicated this whole thing is, this book has a bunch of graphs and charts and tables at the back measuring this stuff. So it's a scientific fact: Loyalty affects behavior.[8]

# My Family

**The one thing I** can pass along with some degree of certainty is that family loyalty is the highest form of loyalty that human beings can give to each other in everyday life. We have talked about the importance of instinct. Well, we know instinctively that our family is going to stick with us long after everyone else has abandoned us. They are going to be the first to come in and help us in a jam, and the last to give up on us.

I grew up believing that the family was the most important thing other than God; the most important thing imaginable. Ours was a very big family. I was the oldest of eight kids. You will assuredly learn something about loyalty if you grow up in a family that size. The first thing you learn is to stick with your siblings because that's who you live with (or have to live with, depending on how you look at it). They are the people who know things you've done and the people who can get you into trouble. There is a kind of Mutually Assured Destruction that goes on there. Of course, you don't only learn about loyalty from what your siblings will do to you if you're disloyal, you learn it by example from your parents.

My Daddy was an incredibly loyal man. He was proud too, but we always had a lot more name than we had money. He was very loyal to the inheritance that was his store in Carville, Louisiana, but he was loyal to it to a fault, to an extreme extent, and I think it affected his health. When I grew up, Carville consisted of two stores. There was ours, which was the L. A. Carville General Merchandise, Carville, Louisiana, and the Geymard store. At a certain point the Geymard store was closed, and now ours is no longer there either. My great-grandmother had run the Carvilles' store, my granddaddy had it, then my Daddy had it, and it was a source of pride to him that the store had been in the family for so long.

In the mid-1960s or so, the economic winds started to blow in a different direction. My father and grandfather were very aggressive in pushing for the new road to Baton Rouge, which cut the driving time by 40 percent. Thanks to innovations like this, people became more mobile. They got around more and they were discovering supermarkets, five-and-dimes, and hardware stores that were more plentiful and cheaper than a country general store like ours.

The profitability of our store declined. We tried to encourage our Daddy to pursue a different route: sandwiches and beer, bread and milk. More of a convenience store. But he resisted. He said we provided a service to the community. The farmers had a place to buy fence nails and the like. To him, that was Carville, and the store was part of the community.

He tried to keep the store going and I really think it led him to an early grave. He worked too hard and worried too much. Someone bought the place and they had to close it. Carville has no stores now. It's a place with a great past. Which is a fancy way of saying it doesn't have a great future. So my father had a misplaced loyalty to the tradition that the store represented. You can't buck an economic trend to that extent. But his tremendous sense of loyalty was a wonderful thing for us in every other respect when we were growing up. We knew that he loved his family desperately.

As far as my attitude toward my father is concerned, I went through a metamorphosis over a long period of time. I think this happens to a lot of people. There was a time, when I was young, that I knew my Daddy was right about everything. Then there was a time when I was a teenager that I thought he was wrong all the time. Now that I'm a parent myself, I'm beginning to believe he might have been right about a lot after all.

I remember when I was seventeen and I was going to New Orleans for the evening. He didn't really have an objection to that. He just said, "Why are you going down to New Orleans? It's hard to find a parking place and a beer costs six bits and you can get a beer for two bits here." It didn't dawn on him why a seventeen-year-old would have any interest in going to Bourbon Street.

My parents were strict in knowing where I was and that I was okay, but my Daddy didn't berate us with stories about how your hands were going to fall off if you masturbated and your life was going to end if you drank beer. He was just mystified as to why any seventeen-year-old would drive an hour and fifteen minutes to New Orleans. Just seemed like a lot of trouble—a long ride for a short beer.

Now, my mother, Miss Nippy—she was much stricter than my father was. He was like me—I hate disciplining my children. They had eight kids. Sometimes my dad would come home and my mom would say, "You got to do something. I just can't take it anymore," and he would line us up and say, "I'll beat the hell out of every one of you," and he'd just burst out laughing.

Miss Nippy was remarkable in her loyalty to her children. I am one half of what she was about sticking with my friends and sticking it to my enemies. If she didn't like someone, she just never let up on them. It would go on for years. When she stuck with something, she really stuck with something. And when she stuck it to someone, she really stuck it to them. She was a sticker both ways.

My mother was absolutely always there for me. I was the world's worst college student. They kicked me out for poor grades and she showed up and bitched and screamed and cried till they let me back into school. When we were young we thought that Miss Nippy was just sort of myopic, but I sure don't think that now. I also used to think that it drove everybody else crazy. One of my cousins, and this was recently, came to me and said, "We were always jealous that your mother stuck up for you and bragged on you all."

(Like any mother, she thought her children hung the moon. One of the lessons I learned is that you can never tell anyone something too nice about their children. You can say some-

**Editors' Note:** In the interests of balance, we called James's sister Pat to see if she had any stories about him. James was very good at securing his family's loyalty, she told us. When he was about sixteen and she was about six, Pat caught James out behind the shed smoking a cigarette. To make sure she wouldn't tell on him, James had Pat take a puff on the cigarette so she was implicated too. Nice, James. Pat was the sixth out of the eight kids. She remembers sitting at the Carville breakfast table: "Who's going to get picked on today? we'd be thinking. Oh, it's Mary Anne today, and I'd join in. We'd really go at it at the breakfast table. But once we left the house, you try and say anything against any of us and we'd be all together."

Pat recalled how James really tested his sister Bonnie's loyalty when they were at LSU. Bonnie was the second child and she and Pat and James were at LSU together. "Everyone was there with James, he was there for so long," Pat says. "Bonnie just started and some guy comes up to her and says, 'You're Bonnie Carville—is your brother James Carville?' 'Yes, he is,' says Bonnie. 'Well, that son of a bitch mooned me last week. He's just a terrible guy.' So whenever people came up to us at LSU after that and said, 'Is James Carville your brother?' we'd say, 'Why do you want to know?' "[1]

thing too nice about someone's spouse or someone's parents, but you can never say anything too nice about someone's children. People are willing to believe anything, and I have demonstrated it. If you ever want something from someone, slobber over their children. I got that from my mother. She would not hear anything bad about her children, and she loved hearing her own view of them confirmed.)

My parents certainly didn't encourage everyone in the family to run out of sight as soon as they could. Pretty much the whole family has stuck with the area. I am the only one to leave southern Louisiana. Actually, other than one sister, I'm the only one to leave the Baton Rouge area, the Baton Rouge television market. One of my sisters lives in Lockport, sixty-five miles away. They certainly do not suffer from any of the disconnects that we have talked about.

An example. My brother-in-law Sparky works for a huge engineering firm. In the 1980s, during the "Massachusetts Miracle," the office in Baton Rouge was not doing very well, and the office in Massachusetts was doing great. My sister said they offered Sparky a whole bunch of money and a big promotion to move up North and she said, "What kind of people do they think we are? Do they think that we would just up and move and leave my mother and my brothers and sisters and everything?" I said to her, "Honey, I've got to tell you, 99 percent of the population is like that. We're a mobile nation out there. You get a promotion and you move." She was taken aback that this company could buy them out of their home. She lives three blocks from one sister in a place where my cousin is the priest and my other sister's the religion teacher at the Catholic school. You're not going to pull her out of there with a winch truck.

My family doesn't understand why I moved away in the first place. They didn't think I was a whole person until I got married anyway. Only once I got married was I whole to them, which means that as far as they were concerned I was only a rounded individual when I was forty-nine.

When I did finally get married, people would ask me about my wife and our, shall we say, political disagreements. And this is what I say: There are people that are married who are of different religions. They hate each other's religion. There are people that are married who share children from one of their previous marriages and they don't get along with those children. There are people who are married who detest each other's in-laws. I just find it easier to be married to a woman who hates my politics than someone who hates my mother. I just love my wife, and if anyone can't deal with that, that's their problem.

If truth be known, I don't think anyone could have a more loyal spouse than I do in Mary. She is fiercely protective of me. She might nag or boss me about sometimes a bit more than I'd like, but she really is the best wife anyone could have. And more importantly, there couldn't possibly be a better mother than she is to our two girls.

After all is said and done, your family is your family whatever they say or think or feel or do. You can't just stop being related to someone. Now, my grandmother had terrible views on race. She would use awful words. I don't think this means she was a bad person. I think she was a good person. I think she was wrong. She had a view on things, and particularly black people, that was bred out of something horribly wrong. She was the product of an age, and it was a philosophy that I rejected relatively early on in life. I didn't follow her on that, but I loved her all the same.

Boy, when I went to bed at night did she make sure I was warm and well fed. You'd better believe it. And when I woke up in the morning was I the king of the house? She always pulled me aside and told me that out of all of her grandchildren, I was her big boy. And she was the best cook in the world.

When I got a bit older, I began to sense there was something wrong with what she said. Now I am sure she was wrong. But I loved her desperately, and I still do. She died thirty years ago or something and I still miss her. What is the more important thing here? The fact that I am loyal to the memory of one of the members of my family, or the fact that it might make me disloyal to other people? I don't know.

This is not what I remember about her. If I knew someone and they espoused the same views that my grandmother did, I probably would not be friends with them. But she was my grandmother. If my grandmother had gone into one of her racist rants, which she did on any number of occasions, I would have gone and put my arm around her, even if she had done it in front of a group of liberals.

My Daddy did say something to her once. We were at my grandmother's house and she was into one of her not infrequent diatribes against black people and was using the N-word. Now, I had never heard my father answer his mother back on any occasion. But this time he said, "Mamma, I really wish you wouldn't use that kind of language around the children," and she said, "Well, son, it's my house, and I'll use the kind of language I want to," and he said, "Well, they're my children." To the extent that it was humanly possible in his mind to stand up to his mother, he had done that. She accommodated him for a good ten or fifteen minutes. At the time I thought it was a heroic act. I must have heard the N-word about a million times before I was eighteen. You would have to live in that era to understand what it was like then, but he did answer her back.

Adults were never criticized in front of children. I remember a story about my Aunt Fanny. She talked a lot—jabbered all the time. Wouldn't shut up for a minute. My grandma was fixing me breakfast and Aunt Fanny was just sitting there and going and going. "Look at that," "Take your time, eat slow," blah, blah. My grandpa was reading the morning paper. He folded the paper down and he said, "Now, Fanny, just be quiet and let the child eat his breakfast." He went back to reading and the force of those words through that kitchen—everything paused for about ten seconds, and she just got up and left right after that. In our family, that was a staggering event.

Some families are faced with much harder problems than getting Aunt Fanny to shut up. What do you do if you are a parent and you think your kid is mixed up in drugs or something? Do you go into your kids' rooms and read their diaries? There are a lot of people that say that you should. That's a decision about loyalty. You trust the kid, but you worry about them and you know they don't want you in looking at their stuff. Where is the line? The line is probable cause. If the kid is going around like a zombie and running around with other zombies, at that point you look for the dope.

Misty Bernall, the mother of Cassie, one of the children murdered at Columbine High School in Littleton, wrote a book about her daughter. Cassie was only at Columbine because she had been pulled from another school in ninth grade. Her mother had gone into her room to look for a Bible and found a bunch of letters from a friend. The friend wrote about killing their parents, about drugs, alcohol, vampires, and self-mutilation; terrible stuff like that. The mother felt her life was in danger, called the police, and got a restraining order against the other girl. But the parents of the other child thought the Bernalls were overreacting and Cassie gave them hell for months. She felt betrayed. There'd been other signs that their daughter was drifting, but the Bernalls only realized how much when they read the letters.[2] But they were tough, and they got it straightened out.

Sometimes, things get so bad, loyalties are stretched to the breaking point. People are stuck between a rock and a hard place and they make decisions that seem to go against the loyalty instinct that we have talked about. These are the crises that seem to turn the whole spectrum of loyalty upside down and that are most striking when they can't be kept within the family.

Let's take the case of the Unabomber's brother. An incredibly traumatic case of divided loyalties. This is worth looking at in detail. The Unabomber was Ted Kaczynski. A Harvard graduate who taught math at Berkeley, Kaczynski turned against the technological world and, in 1978, started mailing letter bombs to people. He killed people and maimed people and the FBI mounted a huge operation to catch him. But he was only caught because his brother, David, told the FBI that he thought the Unabomber might be his brother, Ted. The FBI went and arrested him in 1996 in his cabin in Montana and all they had to start with was the brother's tip-off.

You remember the Unabomber's manifesto? When it was published, David's wife, Linda, who'd never met Ted, joked that he might be the guy and made her husband read the screed. The family was on *60 Minutes* five months after the arrest.[3] David said he agonized for months about contacting the FBI. He hadn't seen his brother for nine years. Whenever he had suggested meeting up, Ted had said no. David and Linda realized that two times, about six weeks after they'd mailed him money, someone got a letter bomb. Finally, David found an essay in a trunk that Ted had written twenty-five years before and it sounded similar to the manifesto. So, through a lawyer, David laid out what he suspected to the FBI.

And about the worst thing was having to tell his mother, who wasn't in the best of health, not only that it was likely that her son was the infamous Unabomber, but also that her other son had turned him in. On *60 Minutes*, David and Ted's mother, Wanda, said:

*He proceeded to tell me and he was walking back and forth and the tears started raining down his face. . . . I realized I knew that David loved his brother and he always had so I knew that what he had done he hadn't done lightly.*

It just got worse when Janet Reno decided to press for the death penalty against Ted Kaczynski. To his family, Kaczynski was a sick man who needed help, not someone who should be executed. And in 1998, the sentence was pled down to a life sentence.

Now, for David Kaczynski this clearly is a case of divided loyalties. He was divided between his own brother and the safety of strangers. This was a truly rending decision, like something out of the Bible. David had to reach deep down and go against the strong ties of family. As he said on *60 Minutes:*

*Certainly one of the things that made my decision very, very difficult was realizing, trying to imagine how it must feel to him to be turned in by his own brother, the only person who had been close to him for a long, long time.*

Now, when all is said and done, David Kaczynski looks like a good guy to me—a very brave guy. He made the decision because people were dying and being crippled. His loyalty to strangers, to people he didn't know who might be murdered and orphaned, was greater than that to a brother. I don't know if I could be that brave. We just have to thank God and pray that we're never put in a position like that by a member of our family. If our loyalties are strongest to our family, it follows that the divided loyalties that can exist where the family is concerned are the most intense as well.

But you have to accept that and it's not something you have to think about every day. The benefits of a tight, loyal family that sticks together are huge. And these benefits are something that can be enjoyed every day. I cherish my family and the strength we draw from each other.

Families are getting smaller and people are getting married later. As I mentioned, I did not get married to Mary until I was forty-nine. When our youngest daughter was born our combined age was something like ninety-six. We now have two kids. I come from a big family—four times as many children as we have—and there is a lot to be said for them. (You can see a picture of the whole family on the jacket of this book.) I'm not preaching or saying that everyone should have a large family, but I'm sure glad I came from one.

But when I was a kid I would complain about it. Around December I used to say to my Daddy, "I wish I had fewer brothers and sisters because there would be more for me at Christmas." He played along with me and said, "We can solve that easily. We can just give them less and give you more. You are the oldest, after all." I was pretty selfish, but not quite bad enough to pursue that particular idea.

Well, this is the way I look at the family now. I am an older parent with two really young kids. I may not be a genius, but I am smart enough to know that things can go wrong in this world. And the level of comfort that I have knowing that I have five sisters and two brothers at home, and that my wife has a sister who lives nearby, is immeasurable. It is better than any life insurance policy or mutual fund. If something happens to me and my wife, then our families are going to be able to take care of our children. The bigger the family, the more people you have for that.

My mother raised eight children and she now has advanced Alzheimer's. She is living at home with my sister who is a nurse. Every night a member of my family stays with her to take care of her. I think of all the diapers she changed for us, all the meals she made for us, all the encyclopedias she sold for us so that we could go to school. Alzheimer's is unforgiving and hard. But I know that she is having as good a quality of life as is possible under the circumstances. That is a result of being from a big family.

So there is something to be said for big families. Big families breed loyalty. There is never a question about it. It is assumed. And if my wife and I were killed in a plane crash tomorrow, I have no doubt that my children would have as good an upbringing as any kid who is not being brought up by their own parents. That is an enormous comfort and brings me tremendous peace of mind.

# My Friends

**I learned an important** lesson about friendship pretty early in life. My first good friend in Carville was John Bernard (J. B.) Engler, known as Bubbie. We would watch the ballgames on television together with his grandfather. They were very loyal Americans. When they were all there, his family would stand up during the National Anthem before the game. His mother, Miss Margarite, loved to make rice and gravy every Sunday and she would let me be the first to eat when I was there. My nickname was "Riley" after a TV show I liked called *The Life of Riley* with William Bendix. The Englers may not have had a great house but it was a great home.

One summer, my cousins came down to stay. I can't remember the year, but I was about eleven or twelve years old. They stayed at my grandmother's and I went and played with them the whole three weeks they were there. Then they left, and I went back to play with Bubbie, and he'd spent the three weeks by himself. He said, "You left me on my own for three weeks and you come over expecting everything to be fine and I gotta say, it's not. I'm kinda hurt."

My cousins had come for three weeks out of the year and I had the other forty-nine with Bubbie. That was a good life lesson. This stuff wasn't around then, but you ask yourself, Are you going to be a Teflon friend or a Velcro friend? It was a two-day thing—we got over it in a couple of days, but it was a tough two days. He's still a great guy. I think he's worked for the same company for thirty years, been married to the same woman thirty years. And the same principles definitely apply whether you're eleven or fifty-five: Teflon or Velcro? If someone is your friend, then they're your friend. You've got to stick with them and maintain the friendship. It's a full-time, two-way thing.

I've said this a thousand times—the worst thing you can lose is a friend. If you lose some money you can work to get your money back, or if you lose your watch you can get another one. But friends are different. In life, you have few real friends. Before you give one up, you better be damn sure it's worth it. Every time I've fallen out with someone, it's been extremely painful and I've missed that person a great deal. I'm very tolerant: I'll go to pretty good extremes to keep a friend because I don't have so many that I can just throw one away and not notice. Benjamin Franklin had something good to say on this subject: "Be slow in choosing a friend, slower in changing."

Sometimes, you screw a friend and it comes back to haunt you. I had a friend named Rudy who was a bookmaker. To put it delicately, I transacted some business with him. There was a two- or three-hundred-dollar debt that I frankly and honestly completely forgot about. My life moved on and Rudy died.

Well, my picture was in the paper or something and his sister saw it and she wrote me a letter. She said she'd been trying to get some money together for her brother's funeral and she'd seen the books and he and I had some business. It was very delicately done. So I sent her the money and the interest. Life can be simple: If you were going to be there on Monday to collect, you'd better be there on Monday to pay up. Sometimes it all comes back and taps you on the shoulder.

For our purposes, there is not a lot of philosophizing to be done about friendship. It is fairly simple: Loyalty defines friendship. One of the things that means is that when everything is going right, you have a lot of friends. It's easy to stick with someone who is doing well. It's amazing how many more friends I have after a client wins an election. If you decide you like someone, that's not conditional on their job or how much money they happen to have in the bank. You stick with them no matter what.

To be friends with someone, you don't have to agree about everything. We don't have to like the same teams or the same music or have the same politics. As I've said before, I've got a lot of friends in Washington. Some of them are even Republicans. Hell, if I can be married to a Republican I sure can be friends with one. As another one of our wise Founding Fathers, Thomas Jefferson, said, "I never considered a difference of opinion in politics, in religion, in philosophy, as cause for withdrawing from a friend."

You know your friend because he or she is the person who

comes and pulls you out of the pile in seventh grade recess. As you grow up, it's the same. I mean it hardly matters how your friend voted or what teams they like or who their other friends are. What's important is that they're saving you from getting stomped on in a bar or lending you money to get your car fixed.

Of all the things that we're going to talk about in this book, friendship is about the most personal. You can't choose your family other than your spouse and the biggest part of that is friendship. You can't choose the country you're born in. You can choose the kind of toothpaste you buy, but that's not going to come up on the Day of Reckoning. In many cases your convictions are so deep-rooted that it seems like they picked you. Remember what Bob Casey said about his father's obligations. But a choice of friends is different.

I'm not going to bore you and talk about how great my friends are. You don't even care who my friends are. But there is one guy I want to talk about and that's my friend George Stephanopoulos. Now, George and I have been through a lot together over the last few years. We worked together on the first Clinton campaign. We were together a lot, a really large part of a lot of days, and we saw the whole thing through side by side. He became, and remains, a friend. Now, a couple of years ago George left the White House and went to work in television and wrote a book that some people criticized him for. This is what I want to say about George.

When I was practicing law in Baton Rouge, I had a case in the City Court, and I discovered that I also had another matter

pending in the District Court which was a little more complicated. I went to the City Court and asked to have this matter
put off so I could take care of this thing in the District Court. I
was waiting and they were calling the different cases up and a
man by the name of Mr. Sam D'Amico, who was a well-
respected longtime attorney in Baton Rouge, was in front of a
judge by the name of William Hawk Daniels.

Mr. D'Amico went to the judge and said, "Your Honor, in a
matter pending before the court, the *City of Baton Rouge v. Jones,*
I would ask the court's indulgence for a continuance for a
period of three weeks because concurrent with this I have a
case pending in the District Court that involves a more complicated piece of litigation. If this does not inconvenience the
court, it's a relatively minor matter and the witnesses that are
here today will be here three weeks from now." And the judge
says, "Granted, Mr. D'Amico."

So they call my case and I say, "Your Honor, in a matter
pending before the court, the *City of Baton Rouge v. Smith,* I
would beg the court's indulgence for a continuance for a period
of three weeks. I have a matter pending in the District Court
that is a little more complicated with more witnesses and other
lawyers. If the court will allow, the same witnesses that are here
today will be here three weeks from now."

The judge says: "Motion denied."

And I said, "Excuse me, Your Honor, but Mr. D'Amico just
made the same argument I did, and you granted his request
and you denied mine."

And he said, "Mr. Carville, Mr. D'Amico is a friend of mine.

103

## With Friends Like These . . .

We can't write a book about loyalty, and have a section about friends, without mentioning Linda Tripp. Of course, Linda Tripp did things in the name of friendship that kind of blow the mind. On the *Today* show, Katie Couric asked me about Linda Tripp. The point I wanted to make then is, I don't know how she grew up, what she grew up with. I do know this: We are just two different people. It would be hard to imagine, politically, anybody whose outlook on the world is so fundamentally different from mine. I don't think Linda Tripp as a person is bothered by stabbing anyone in the back. People have said that the ultimate punishment for Linda Tripp is that she has to live with herself. I don't really have anything to add to that.

You're not. To deny a friend is to deny Christ. Surely you are not asking me to sit on this bench and deny Christ. Are you? Is that what you're asking me?"

That's it. That's all I want to say. He's a friend of mine. I'm not going to fall out with someone who has a different take on something. I'm not a tyrant. He has his take, I have my own take, and that's it. He's a friend and I'm sticking with him.

**By this** point, somebody reading this book might be tempted to ask, "James, you talk about loyalty, you tell us about how you grew up, and you give us all of these observations, but what about loyalty to your wife? What about what Bill Clinton did to Hillary Clinton? Did that disturb you?"

And the answer is, of course it did. The pain and agony it caused his wife and daughter is, frankly, something I would rather not contemplate. But there's a difference between doing something that causes pain and agony to your own family and actually abandoning them. And if it is a friend who has caused this pain to his family, there is a lot you can do short of turning your back on him. There are more ways of showing your displeasure than stabbing a guy in the back. Particularly if it is a friend who has done a lot for you. Your reaction should be proportional to the offense.

But was I angry about what the president put his family through? Of course. No one who had seen the president's wife on the day he testified could fail to sense the pain. But to tell you the truth, I did not have much time to get mad at him because of all the idiots screaming in my face right away. I was too busy being mad at the right-wingers and all the jerks in the press.

A few people like to make a point about what they think the president did to me and his other friends. These individuals say, "James, Bill Clinton didn't tell you the truth. And friends are not supposed to lie to friends." I would say that a person who says something like that is a jerk. Because I wouldn't expect anyone to tell a friend about anyone they had sex with. I certainly don't expect anyone to tell me about it.

As a matter of fact, where I come from, it is sometimes considered honorable to lie about sex. Only a dishonorable person would tell the truth about it. Most people follow this rule about sex: Those that say they did, didn't, and most who say they didn't, did. You will be right about 75 percent of the time if you go by that formula. Anyway, if the main thing I have to get over in my life is a friend fibbing to me about sex, then I have had a pretty easy time of it.

# In the Name
# of God

**Loyalty to God is,** along with loyalty to country, the most revered kind of loyalty. These are loyalties that are not related to a person, something that interacts with you. You can quantify the time and emotional energy you put into your faith, but what you get back is not measurable in any way. Most people in America say they believe in God. But every person who believes takes something different from their relationship with God. Each relationship is unique. I wouldn't presume to comment on individual faith and what people believe even if I could. But I can say that while there is no one right way to demonstrate your loyalty to God, there sure are a lot of wrong ways.

The best known story of disloyalty and treachery of all is in the Bible. One of the first people I thought of when I began this book was Judas Iscariot. As I thought about the story of Jesus' Crucifixion, I realized the significant thing about it is not Judas's act of treachery. He was a greedy person who was bought off with his thirty pieces of silver. The more meaningful character is Peter, who denied Jesus three times.

The remarkable thing about Peter is that Jesus knew he was going to betray him, he did it, and Jesus forgave him. Jesus predicted it and Peter did it anyway. And we know that Saint Peter is the rock upon which the church was built—the founder of the Christian religion, the first saint. Jesus was being loyal to his friend even in the face of being denied three times. And I thought, What does that say about how hard it is to stick with someone? I think that's the important thing here. To my mind this is Jesus' way of saying that we all have some treachery in us.

To me, if demonstrating loyalty to God can be boiled down to one thing, it's in Matthew 7:12. "All things whatsoever ye would that men should do to you, do ye even so to them: for this is the law and the prophets." To me, this is the most profound piece of morality that anyone has given in the history of the world. Basically it says do as you would be done by. If this is all we ever took from our allegiance to God and really applied it in our daily lives and stuck with it, we'd be a lot better off. Think about it and you'll realize how infrequently it is observed. We're much more likely to just see what we can get away with. This isn't what we're supposed to be doing.

Most Americans profess to be demonstrating loyalty to the same God, but in reality we are picking and choosing. We now vest God with anything we want. It's like a giant cafeteria. There's a Piccadilly Cafeteria in Baton Rouge and you go down the line and you take a piece of pie if you like the look of it but if you don't like the look of something you don't take it. People treat God like that. (There is a kind of Catholic called a

cafeteria Catholic. That's me. You can leave out papal infallibility, the proscription on birth control, and some other stuff as
far as I'm concerned.)

The right uses God to hate everybody and everything and
they ignore the parts of the Bible that don't fit. (It reminds me
of the Republican impeachment managers and their copies of
the Constitution.) A bit more adherence to that line from
Matthew would shut most of them up right away. The way to
be loyal to God is to lead the life and to shut your mouth.

I believe that the God my parents taught me about and the
God the nuns at my school taught me about is deserving of my
loyalty and fidelity. When we talk about loyalty to God, I am
not about to tell you, dear reader, which version of God is the
right one—whether it's the Judaic God or the Christian God or
the Islamic God or the God of Righteousness. For me, in the
end, I like the God of Mother Robert at St. Joseph's parochial
school that I was acquainted with growing up. That God never
told me to hate anybody or anything.

I am probably not afflicted with the degree of certainty I
ought to be, even as I am approaching old age. I have never
used God as an excuse to hurt anybody, be cruel to anyone, or
set myself off to think I'm better than another person. If you
do these things, don't blame God or give God the credit for
your cruelty or your mendacity or your pettiness or your narrow-
mindedness or your bigotry.

Now, I'm not setting myself up as some great paragon of
religious virtue here. There's a passage in the Bible that tells us
that if someone comes up to you and asks for your shirt, you're

not supposed to give them your shirt, you're supposed to give them your coat. But if I'm going to be loyal to Jesus, I must say that I have never given my coat. I've never given a new coat at any rate. You can have my old high school letter jacket, but you can't have my Burberry's. And loyalty to a religion is different from loyalty to God. When Notre Dame plays SMU, I'll like Notre Dame because I'm a Catholic. (But when Notre Dame plays LSU, I pull for LSU.) But that's not what loyalty to God is about.

Loyalty to God can obviously be a powerful positive force. Faith can get someone through a difficult time in their life. Billions upon billions of hours and of dollars in charity are spent to help people. People of incredible character work to alleviate human suffering with a level of human goodness that it is almost impossible for us to understand. Not just because I am an adherent do I say this, but there probably has been no faith in the history of the world that has produced more of this than the Christian faith.

But let's not kid ourselves, folks: A lot of people have done a lot of bad professing to be loyal to God too. We have seen cases where an individual will invoke the name of God to justify bombing an abortion clinic. Many millions of people have been killed in the name of loyalty to God in religious wars over the centuries. Religious zealots killing people for God clearly suffer from too much loyalty.

So while I think I have been loyal to God in my own way, I can say that we have been let down on occasion by the institutions of the church and their representatives and what they have done over the centuries. Actually, they didn't let me down as much as devastate my faith when I found out about some of these things. While I express loyalty to the Vatican, do I express loyalty to the Inquisition? And what about Pope Pius XII? He was the formative spiritual influence that I grew up with. He was a venerated man. Now look at what they're saying about him. The recent best-seller about him was called *Hitler's Pope*, which makes a compelling case that Pius XII was not all he was cracked up to be.[1]

There's something going on here that has me very disturbed and I hope I can work my way through it. *Hitler's Pope* is by an English Catholic called John Cornwell. It's about the pope in the Second World War and how he made accommodations with the Nazis. The best defense I can come up with, which is by stretching to great lengths, is that he was a very, very pragmatic man who was very loyal to the power of the papacy and didn't think much of democracies or liberals. That is the most charitable explanation for what he did I can come up with.

I cannot believe that the current pope advocates canonizing Pius XII. Some people must be advising the Holy Father because it's out on the table. There's not a lot of things that I am sure of in this world, but I am about as certain as one human being can be that Pius XII does not have any business being made a saint of the Roman Catholic Church. This is not the stuff of which saints are made; this is the stuff pragmatic politicians are made of. Does all this mean I'm going to reject my Church? I doubt it. But I am very troubled by this and deeply embarrassed. I just wish some of this embarrassment would be felt by the people in the Vatican who are advising the pope to canonize this guy.

This reminds me of one of the great revelations I had in life. I grew up in a very Catholic household. In Catholic school they taught us, shall we say, a very slanted view of the Reformation. Our Church was holy; the Protestants were out of line. "We're right, they're wrong," I guess you could say. I never thought about it, I just had a view of it that I'd been taught and I went along with it.

When I was forty-six years old I went to Rome with my friends Bob Shrum and Mary Louise Oates. It took me all of five minutes in that city to understand why the Reformation took place. You just look at all that ostentation. You cannot go to Rome and have a brain and not understand the Reformation. I mean these boys got flat out of hand. Clearly the people in the Reformation had a point. Instinctively, my first reaction was, "Uh-oh." In one moment, forty-six years of certainty crumbled in front of me. I felt like John Belushi in the dean's office in the movie: forty-six years down the drain. I hadn't gone to Rome in search of any great truths, I was in Rome searching for a good time: some good food and some history.

But I can say that, for me, there is a God that I remember and cherish from parochial school. As I have gotten older, I've seen things and heard about things and read things that show me that my loyalty to God does not extend to embracing all the views and actions of the Catholic Church and does not extend to embracing all the views and actions of those people who say they are Christians. That would be blind loyalty, which is either sycophancy or stupidity or both. It's just another example of how much more complicated things get the more you look into them.

So am I a better Catholic at fifty-five than I was at fifteen? Probably not. But am I a better Catholic at fifty-five than I was at twenty-five? Probably so. I think I understand at some level that the Church is a human institution. It's not infallible. It's a mistake to assert that. Any honest Catholic I have ever spoken to thinks infallibility is a mistake. It's a mistake, so why don't we just say it? It was a mistake in its conception, it was a mistake to bring it about, and it's a mistake to maintain it. It's not as much of a mistake as creationism, but it's still a mistake.

While we're on that subject, this is another thing done in the name of God that I want to stop. I don't want to pay tax money to give someone a voucher to learn that the earth is five thousand years old. I don't think it's wrong, I know it's wrong. It's just wrong. I'm not even a scientist, I'm not even an intellectual. I'm not even smart. The fundamentalists are loyal to the Bible to the point of being asinine. If they think God is going to give them any credit for their narrow-mindedness and stupidity, they're crazy.

We should look at all of these failings in context. We should remember all of the sick people that the church has cared for and comforted; we should recall the children it has educated and looked after, the hungry it has fed, the naked it has clothed, and the souls it has saved. The totality of the picture tells me that the church is absolutely worthy of the loyalty of its members. Of course, being loyal to something doesn't mean that you can't disagree with it from time to time, and I have. I think I disagree most when the church gets involved in politics and not when it is caring for its members. But these disagreements pale when set against the good things that have been done over the centuries.

So you can see that my religious loyalty has limits. Because it's about a faith that has been thought about and principles that have stood the test of time and changed a bit, it's not such an instinctual thing anymore. It might have been when I was fourteen, when I thought the Church was right about everything. But I think I have stuck with the basic elements of my faith.

I now realize that people invoke the name of God all the time to validate their terrible views. The God of Pat Robertson, Jerry Falwell, Bob Barr, and Tom DeLay. The God that the Council of Conservative Citizens and the KKK are big into. I don't know that God and I don't care to meet him. I think it's an affront to God to be slinging around biblical quotes like these guys do. Do you think that God really has an opinion on whether you should vote for a tax cut or not? Whatever God is or whoever he is, I think we can agree that he doesn't want credit from Mr. Falwell for his hating gay people or credit from the right-wing Republicans for his hating Bill Clinton.

Let's talk about Jerry Falwell for a minute. I know you'd probably rather not, but I'm sorry, we have to. He has a pretty nice business in Lynchburg, Virginia, built around his relationship with God. He has the Thomas Road Baptist Church he began in 1956, a school, a university, his *Old-Time Gospel Hour*, a

TV station, a radio station, the *National Liberty Journal,* and a well-stocked online store where a percentage of each purchase goes to the Jerry Falwell Ministries. He's clearly extremely loyal to God. So much so that he seems to expect special treatment in return. In 1994, the basketball team from his Liberty University played North Carolina in the first round of the NCAA tournament. Dean Smith mentions this in his autobiography.

*Dr. Falwell said before the game he was confident his team could do well against us, even though we were ranked number one in the nation, and he asked God to lead his team to victory. It was almost as if the reverend was saying that his team had some extra weapons they could throw at us. When a writer asked me to comment on Falwell's plea to the Almighty, I merely said, "I think God loves all humans the same."*[2]

I couldn't agree more. Every time I see an athlete say "God helped me make the shot" or "Jesus helped me throw a strike," it makes me crazy. It's moronic. As if God helped him put the ball in the hoop or made sure he got the ball over the plate. A belief in God may help someone fulfill his or her potential as an athlete, but it's not as though God likes one team better than another. Are you saying you're a better person than the person guarding you? People don't score goals or win elections because God wants them to.

Let me say this about Jerry Falwell. I said it about someone else once: I wouldn't piss down that son of a bitch's throat if his heart was on fire. Now, you understand that this is just a turn of phrase—I don't want anything bad to happen. I don't want

Jerry Falwell to get sick or anything, I just want him to shut up. (Well, maybe I wouldn't be too upset if he stubs his toe.) He is one of the world's really bad people.

This is worth looking into a little. Remember, what we are talking about here is loyalty to God. I think we can trust most people to be able to recognize godliness when they encounter it. Racial segregation was something that existed in this country that I think we can agree was an affront to God, let alone to man. Jerry Falwell has said that he repudiated segregation in probably 1963 or 1964, but he was still criticizing the civil rights movement in 1965. Nineteen sixty-five, not 1865. He gave a sermon at his Thomas Road Baptist Church in Lynchburg on March 21, 1965, in which he spoke about civil rights and segregation:

*I do question the sincerity and non-violent intentions of some civil rights leaders such as Dr. Martin Luther King, Jr., Mr. James Farmer, and others, who are known to have left-wing associations.*

Jesus, he goes on to say, is not interested in politics. Jesus would try to convert people and work on them from the inside out. He quotes John 4:6–14. Jesus asks a Samaritan woman for water. She reminds him that the Samaritans and the Jews don't associate with each other. In effect, they are segregated. Now Jesus could have preached to her about the evils of segregation, says Falwell, but he didn't. Instead, he tries to convert her. Falwell goes on to ask, why don't church leaders talk about discrimination in the North? Or against Native Americans?

Because it's the votes in the South the politicians are after. Falwell goes on, why don't they talk about alcoholism? After all, "There are almost as many alcoholics as there are negroes."[3]

He said that from a pulpit in a church. Again, it's worth saying that Falwell relates to a God that I don't recognize. The forum he decided to use to equate alcoholism and being black was a sermon from a pulpit in a church. This is a guy who has also said that the antichrist is a Jew.[4] He famously got in trouble for anti-Semitism in his campaign against Jimmy Carter. In an "I Love America rally" in Richmond he said, "I know a few of you here today don't like Jews. And I know why. He can make more money accidentally than you can on purpose."[5]

Black people, Jewish people. What's missing? Ah yes, we can all sleep more soundly on our beds at night knowing that Dr. Falwell is still working to rid us of the curse of homosexuality. Let's review a recent posting on Falwell.com:

*We at Jerry Falwell Ministries know that God can break the destructive influence of homosexual acts as you trust in Him and commit to live a godly life.*

Links from Falwell.com take you to "Exodus International," an organization whose given "primary" purpose, according to its Web site, is to "proclaim that freedom from homosexuality is possible through repentance and faith in Jesus Christ." From here one can flip to support groups like "Parents and Friends of Ex-Gays" and "Homosexuals Anonymous," which helpfully provides a fourteen-step program for those wishing to escape

## Me and My Big Mouth!
## Pat Robertson and the Bank of Scotland

Here's a little parable for you. A lot of people have said that I have a big mouth. But at least when I open it, the kind of hate that Pat Robertson spouts doesn't come out.

In March 1999, the Bank of Scotland, a venerable financial institution, announced a deal with Pat Robertson that would bring their financial expertise and his congregation together. Robertson stood to make lots of money. For some reason, he sent a reporter to Scotland and spoke on the *700 Club* about the land of his new business partners. He had discovered a hideous truth: Scotland has gay people living in it. "In Scotland you can't believe how strong the homosexuals are," the great sociologist mused. "And what could happen? It could go right back into the darkness very quickly. . . . I was entranced by the history of that great land, but I think that the modern-day reality is something far, far different from what it used to be."

Needless to say, the Scots were displeased. Hundreds of individuals closed accounts. Institutions threatened to go elsewhere. The TUC, the British AFL-CIO, promised to reconsider an arrangement with the bank. Bill Spiers of the Scottish TUC said, "Mr. Robertson might be kind enough to say that God has not given up on Scotland, but he certainly seems to have given up on Mr. Robertson."[7] The deal was killed.

We know that we're probably not going to get Pat Robertson

to change his hateful views, so the morals of this story are three
in number: Don't go into business with a bigot; Don't bite the
hand that feeds you; and, If you've got nothing good to say, say
nothing.

the clutches of their sexuality. (Question for Jerry: Are there as
many gay people as there are "negroes" or alcoholics?)

All this ridiculous crap is perpetrated in the name of God.
When there is discrimination against gay people, when people are
murdered because they are gay, and countless individuals live
double lives because they feel stigmatized by their sexuality, these
idiots are telling them they're full of sin and need to be saved.

I hope people don't think this phony attempt to soften his
image by talking to gay people is going to change anyone's mind.
What kind of idiots does he take people for? As we saw in our last
book, he's someone who cares that we know what he thinks about
President Clinton, so we should know what he thinks about us.[6]

We could go on with a lot more examples from people like
that. It's clear that the right has always used Christianity as an
excuse for their bigotry. They would say that they are very loyal
to God and that they go to church every Sunday. I'm not certain about much, but I believe this: If it's possible to incur the
wrath of God, then this will do it. Using God's name while
expressing these kinds of views will get his or her dander up
about as much as anything I could imagine.

# My Country

**Patriotism must feature in** any discussion of loyalty. Look back at the dictionary definitions we included and pretty much all of them define loyalty in terms of honoring the country. Americans are very patriotic—we're proud of our country and rightly so. I doubt whether the people in any other country fly flags outside their homes so much, and I bet that nowhere else has there been a constitutional debate on whether it's okay to burn the nation's flag or not.

Obviously, patriotism is most evident and most called upon in wartime. People are asked to be patriotic in times of crisis or war and most citizens respond. Look at the Soviet Union in World War II. That conflict there is called "The Great Patriotic War" and Stalin was clever enough to realize that the patriotism was stirred by the *rodina* (the motherland), not by the Soviet government. He quickly rehabilitated all the old Russian heroes, like Alexander Nevsky, to help people associate a mother Russia they wanted to fight for with his regime.

We can see that it's easy to be patriotic in peacetime—any used-car salesman can run a flag up the pole on July 4th. My experience of patriotism is that it's always the person who has done the least who yells the most. The guy who has the biggest flag has never done a thing and the guy who has won the Medal of Honor never says a word.

Most of the time, when we're not at war, the government kind of is the country, or at least it represents the country. If you live in a democracy you assume that a government has been put legally into place. I mean, am I loyal to the Republican Congress? Not really, but do I follow their laws? Yes. I am loyal to the rule of law. Part of being a loyal citizen is to get involved in the political process and to express dissent. You don't slavishly follow what you're asked to do without thinking about it. But you still drive on the right-hand side of the road because that's the law.

Talking about "my country," we quickly get into some gray areas. My country right or wrong? Well, my country. But how wrong would the country have to be to override that? Well, very wrong. We have to talk about drawing the line again. Where do you draw it? How wrong does the country have to be? You can talk endlessly about this or that circumstance, but it's difficult to talk about hypothetical situations.

In 1933 the students at Oxford University's Union had a debate which passed a motion "that this House will in no circumstances fight for King and Country."[1] Hitler had just come to power and some thought that this showed that England's elites weren't going to stand up to dictators. But England wasn't at war. It's different if there's a foreign invader coming up your driveway with a gun in his hand and a bad look in his eye.

Also in England, the novelist E. M. Forster wrote an essay called "What I Believe" in which he said, "If I had to choose between betraying my country and betraying my friend, I hope I should have the guts to betray my country."[2] He wrote this in 1939, which was the year full-scale war broke out in Europe, but what would the circumstances have to be in which a novelist would be forced to choose between his country and a friend? It's not as though he were chief of staff. I mean, you never really had to decide, Mr. Forster.

In the same vein, the French philosopher Jean-Paul Sartre said if he had to choose between his mother and the French Resistance, he'd choose his mother.[3] These people were intellectuals speculating about philosophical dilemmas. They're interesting to talk about and it was Sartre's job to write about stuff most of us would never think of. That's what he did for a living.

Some people actually make choices like this. Their loyalties are divided and they choose one at the expense of the other. Now, when we are talking about our country, if you are from one country and you decide to operate in the service of another, then that can be treason. Treason is discussed in our Constitution as "adhering to the enemy." So a traitor can only really exist when we have an enemy—when we are at war.

This complicates the spying case of Jonathan Pollard, who spied against the United States but on behalf of Israel. George Fletcher wrote about this in his book. He points out that Israel not only is not an enemy of the United States, but is an ally. A lot of people think Pollard should be let out of jail. Before his sentencing, Caspar Weinberger wrote the judge and called Pollard a "traitor," which, strictly speaking, isn't the case.[4] Whether or not it technically was treason, he was a spy. It seems to me that Pollard was working for the U.S. government and accepting its money. Giving away our secrets, even to an ally, is not loyal and would seem to meet the definition of a crime. He might have been loyal, but he was not loyal to the people who were paying him.

And here's another example of a complicated divided loyalty: If you were a loyal American in the 1770s, it meant you were automatically disloyal to the British Crown, which was, rightly or wrongly, in charge and the authority under the law as it existed. The people that stuck with the Crown were called Loyalists, after all. And the opposition (our side) were the patriots. Fletcher makes the point here that you have a football team called the New England Patriots. You'd never get a team called the New England Loyalists.[5]

Perhaps our most famous patriot is Nathan Hale. In 1776, Hale volunteered for a spying mission behind enemy lines, knowing what the British would do to him if he were discovered. He was caught and hanged on September 22, 1776. His famous dying words were "I only regret that I have but one life to lose for my country." Nathan Hale is rightly revered as a loyal American patriot. He was loyal to his cause and died for it. Even if he was by law a British subject, Nathan Hale was an American patriot.

As we have seen, Robert E. Lee was a man who thought a lot about divided loyalties. After the Civil War, he used an example from the Revolutionary War to justify his own actions. He took the case of George Washington himself:

*At one time [Washington] fought against the French under Braddock in the service of the King of Great Britain; at another, he fought with the French at Yorktown, under the orders of the Continental Congress of America, against him. He has not been branded by the world with reproach for this; but his cause has been applauded.*[6]

As we've said before, life is complicated, and never more so than during wartime. George Washington, like Nathan Hale, is revered for making a choice in a fight. History has judged their cause to be a better one than Lee's.

Other people stick with their beliefs and their cause and they mean that they cannot fight. Like the Mennonites, who are pacifists, who went south to Mexico and Central America at the Civil War and World Wars I and II. I'm not going to say that their loyalty is a lesser one. It's a tough stance to take because conscientious objectors face a lot of stigma. They have to actively stick by their beliefs and take hits for them.

In this country in my lifetime, perhaps in the whole history of the country, the period that created the most divided loyalties, the most schisms, was the Vietnam War. I generally operate on a much less lofty premise than most people. When I joined up, I didn't really think too much about it because I didn't have a choice. I joined a) because I was going to be drafted anyway and b) because it was what the Carvilles always did. We didn't go to Canada. The idea that you were a Carville and that you didn't serve in the military at this time was frankly unthinkable.

My grandfather was a farmer during World War I and he had a lot of kids so he didn't get sent over to France. My dad and all my uncles were in the service. I have a framed newspaper clipping on the wall in my office. It's from the *State Times* of Baton Rouge, Saturday, June 17, 1944. It says that for Father's Day, Major Thomas Blakeney, husband of Mary Pearl Carville, had returned from eighteen months in Africa and Italy and that Major Chester J. Carville, my Daddy, was in from Fort Benning, Georgia. They'd be home but they'd be missing Major Louis A. Carville, who'd been in China twenty-one months; Captain David J. Carville, who'd been in the South Pacific for twenty-six months; and Staff Sergeant Lloyd Carville, twenty, who was with the Air Force in the United Kingdom. He was a tail gunner in a B-17. Reading it makes me very proud.

As a kid, we'd read about Nathan Hale and shoot "Japs" and "Krauts" in games. And as far as we were concerned, there were no bad wars and there were no Carville men who did not go and fight in them. The U.S. is fighting, ergo it must be a good war. So off the Carvilles went to Vietnam: Brother Bill was a soldier in the U.S. Army; Cousin Mike was a Huey pilot; Cousin Bobby was a Navy corpsman serving with the Marines.

Anyway, the main reason I joined the Marine Corps was not that I was desperate to go and fight the Vietnam War. And, thank God, I was not sent off to do that. When I first got to the

Marine Corps Recruiting Depot in San Diego and joined the 1032 Platoon, I did harbor some desire to go to Vietnam because it was a war and young people went to war.

At that point, I wasn't very schooled in the horrors of things. In time, people started coming back and they'd say, "Shut up— that ain't no place you want to go." It became apparent to me that this war was not a good war and that my country had made a bad mistake. They had made a mistake about being there at all, and they were making the mistake worse by sending poor, disadvantaged people in great numbers over there to fight for something that was only vaguely defined. The Vietnam War turned out to be a giant fart in a deep-sea diving suit, a skunk at our patriotic garden party. I had been kind of lollygagging through life and here was this bad war. I mean guys would stick their legs out from behind trees over there trying to get a stateside injury.

So when I heard the sheer volume of wisdom that was being imparted to me, I thought the best of it. I had joined the Marines on June 6, and sometime in February, twenty months later, they called us out on a movement. There's a difference between going AWOL and missing a movement. Going AWOL you can get restricted to quarters, but if you miss a movement you can theoretically get shot. This was a movement, and we were moving my unit over.

They called everyone together and said anyone who has a discharge date prior to June 12 or June 15 or something like that, step aside. A first sergeant came out and said, "Look, the government is too tight to send you bastards over there when

**The Marines** really drill loyalty into you. You learn that once someone is a Marine, they're always a Marine. You're never a former Marine or an ex-corporal or general: You're a Marine. You might greet someone you know was a Marine with "Semper Fi" (from the motto "Semper Fidelis") so you know you're both Marines. Zell Miller wears his Marine Corps pin every day.

While I was glad not to be sent to Vietnam by the U.S. Marines, I give them a lot of credit for the way things turned out for me. Next to my family, they were the most responsible for the turnaround in my life. I think young people are drawn to the Marines today because they want to belong to something they know they can be loyal to. The Marines don't have any problem with recruiting, even when the other services might be struggling a bit.

they would have to bring you back so soon, but I have a deal here: One more stripe plus a $1,200 bonus if you sign up for another three years." He went on to tell me about how good it was and how I should do it and I said, "We can sit here between now and June and I ain't signing nothing." I didn't want to get my ass shot off. The idea of being separated from my ass did not seem particularly attractive to me at the time and I certainly have never regretted not going. What I do profoundly regret and will always regret is that almost sixty thousand Americans lost their lives in Vietnam.

I never knew anyone in the Marine Corps who said, "You really should have gone over there." All of my friends who had been said, "You lucky bastard, I wish I was you." Sometimes it's smart to put a limit on your patriotic fervor. I didn't think Vietnam was any war for me to be doing a Nathan Hale in. I'm glad I was never in a position where my life might be sacrificed for a South Vietnamese government or the "domino effect."

Fast-forward to 1992 and you have all this pontificating about the draft and Bill Clinton's famous draft letter. Most people that I knew were completely torn about the Vietnam War. That a guy who went to Georgetown and Oxford was torn about the war bothered me not in the least. As the whole thing evolved and we saw what was happening it became pretty clear that the people that were against the war were right. All of the people that were the same generation as Governor Clinton and I, they didn't think this was any kind of big deal. It was a generational thing. The middle was not concerned; it was the young and the old who were more concerned about it.

Move forward in time again to the last couple of years and the crisis in Kosovo. Now, I think what our country did there, led by President Clinton, was unequivocally a fine thing and a great service to the whole human race. Countless lives were saved and a dictator was stood up to and made to climb down. Now, I have a strong suspicion that there are people in prominent positions in this country who hated the president so much that they would be more loyal to that than to the country. I suspect that there were people who wanted our mission in Kosovo to fail. This is quite a staggering thing to comprehend.

As I've said throughout this book, life is complicated. We should always recognize that. Vietnam took place at a very complicated time for our country. It's easy to make it all seem simple in retrospect. The closest many of the people who now sound tough about patriotic responsibilities during the 1960s have ever gotten to Vietnam is when they have a prawn roll in a restaurant at home. People's loyalties were pulled every way during that war.

I learned a lot about myself and my country during that period. I found out mostly that I was pretty lucky. I began to wonder if all that stuff they told us in catechism about the guardian angel wasn't true. For a two-year enlistee not to get sent to Vietnam was pretty unusual, so I was fortunate.

After I left the Marines, I went to law school and you know enough of the track I took to know that I ended up in Washington, our capital. I thank God that our patriotism is not tested a great deal in the times we live in. I am happy to be able to support my country in a time of relative peace. Because we have crassly right-wing judges and a judiciary manipulated for no other reason than to screw the president is not enough to make me doubt my country.

# My Politics

**I am a loyal** Democrat. Why? I think, by and large, the Democrats have stuck with the people and the things I care most about: equal opportunity, tolerance, education. I think I do have a personal political philosophy. I don't have the kind of moral certainty on issues that some people have but I do have a sense of where I'd like to see the country go. My politics passes our test of instinctive loyalty. By this time, I don't have to think about it. I'm a Democrat and proud of it.

As opposed to Republicans, who tend to think the world was a much better place back when Strom Thurmond cast his first vote, Democrats are always eager to improve our country. We don't want to sit on the sidelines. But am I absolutely convinced that if you have a dollar, it's better to give that dollar to school construction or a children's tax credit? No, I have to say, I don't know. If you ask me one day I might think one thing, on another day I could very well think another. I believe if most people are honest with themselves, they do this too. They're in that 55–45 area I'm in on the death penalty. I can't tell you the number of times in my life I've heard somebody make an argument and think, Gee, that makes sense, and I heard somebody else stand up and make an entirely different argument and think, Well, that makes sense too.

That makes party political loyalty complicated. I mean, does political loyalty demand that if you're for one thing your party stands for, you have to be for all of them? Because you're for increasing the education budget, does that mean you have to be against a three-day wait for an abortion?

Everyone in Washington says they're fiscal conservatives and social liberals. Deep down inside, I'm probably a fiscal liberal and a social traditionalist, which is another departure from the norms of Washington. I believe that intact families are the strongest foundation for a society. I also believe that the government has an affirmative obligation to provide people with opportunity. I think that the progressive income tax—i.e., those that make more pay a higher rate—is a fundamental principle. (I don't want to say that I'm a "social conservative" because that connotes prejudice to me. I don't want to be associated in any way with that. I don't want anyone to think I'm anti-gay or anti-immigrant.)

If people want to call me a liberal or a progressive, that's okay. But what do they mean? Why can someone in favor of a progressive income tax not be supportive of intact families? If the test for being a liberal is not to be a bigot, then that is not a very tough test for someone to pass. All of this doesn't prevent us Democrats from sharing a sense of direction, a sense of responsibility to make the world better, and being loyal to that

**Probably the** best teacher I ever had was T. Harry Williams, who was Boyd Professor of History at LSU. Williams wrote one of the great political biographies of all time, *Huey Long,* about the legendary Louisianan. There's a great story in the book about Oscar K. "OK" Allen, who was governor of Louisiana. Allen really let people push him around—he'd act pretty much as directed and was a bit of a sycophant, especially toward Huey Long, who had gotten him elected. Huey's brother Earl told a story: Allen was sitting at his desk one day signing state papers when a leaf blew in through the window. Earl said Allen signed the leaf.[1]

ideal. So when my personal political loyalty is put to its biannual test, it's another easy decision for me: I vote the ticket.

Politics is something I make a living at. Anybody that is a political consultant is going to have problems from time to time. It's easy to see you have several competing loyalties. You have a loyalty to earning a living. If you were like me and you weren't getting a lot of work, you couldn't cherry-pick. And like anybody else, you develop a philosophy. If you're working in politics, you've probably thought more about this than an accountant or a gas station attendant, because it's what you do. Now, very seldom do two human beings meet who agree with each other on everything.

Questions that I am often asked are: How do you pick the

candidates you work for? And, do you have to agree with them to work for them? Well, when you work with people on a campaign, you develop a loyalty to them. On election night, what doesn't go through your mind is: This will secure a woman's right to choose for the next four years or classroom size will go from twenty-three to twenty. You feel good because the people you worked with are going to share in the joy that you feel. The people you worked with have succeeded. Not a minor consideration is that you have a chance to sign up with a bigger and better campaign the next time. For more money.

So the question becomes: At what point do you separate from the guy you're working for? When do your personal political loyalties intervene? I worked for Bob Casey, who was pro-life even in the case of rape and incest, and I worked for Frank Lautenberg, who voted for pro-choice legislation. I worked for Zell Miller, who was a death penalty advocate, and for Lloyd Doggett, who opposed the death penalty. Plus, I have had numerous conversations with candidates and found out that they had a position that was different from mine. But many people work for companies and find some policy the company has that they disagree with.

We've already talked about drawing the line and the point at which I would say "Hey, I'm out of here." As far as political opinions are concerned, I think if you found out that the candidate is a bigot you'd have to go, and from a general moral standpoint, if the guy's a crook, you should get out too. There's only one candidate I didn't finish with and that was on the principle that they weren't taking my advice. They were taking somebody else's advice.

Sometimes your party or your people do something that really tests your loyalty. It's not the same thing as what a grown man and a young woman may have done together in private. That is no test of loyalty for me. Unlike any other person in Washington, if you ask me what I think is a bigger wrong, a grown man acting stupid with a young woman and trying to cover it up or cutting legal immigrants off government benefits, to me it's not even a close call. I thought that was a sin against God. If we want to talk about tested loyalty, that was really tested loyalty. I almost did draw the line right there.

I felt sickened by the president when he signed that bill. I think it was a chickenshit thing to do. I can say now that I really wrestled with my relationship with Bill Clinton. I anguished and agonized over it. I was about to jump. And I called the president's adviser Rahm Emanuel about it and I was in tears. George Stephanopoulos was sickened by it too. I know this because of contemporaneous conversations. George went in to see the president after he signed it and said, "Don't you think you ought not to play golf this afternoon?" According to George, the president screamed at him and said George just wanted to wear a hair shirt. I think the president didn't play golf.

Do I think less of Bill Clinton because he signed that bill? The answer is yes. And the reason is that, deep down inside, I think the president knew that the policy was dead-ass wrong and that it was immoral to cut these people off. I'm not so naive that I don't realize there's a political calculation to everything that's done in Washington, but there was too much of a political calculation here and not enough concern for the human element.

The president has talked about the hot-blooded being judged differently than the coldhearted. Fine. I agree. I was the first person in line to forgive him for acting stupid with Monica Lewinsky, for which the Washington Commentariat will be the last people to forgive you. They will be the first to say it was fine to cut off legal immigrants and I will be the last in line on that one.

This is just another example of how I am completely disconnected from Washington. Unlike any pontificator, columnist, commentator, or hot-air jock, I think that the God I know was much more angry about something like that than about the sex. I feel that perhaps it was cowardly of me not to just walk away. That was a principle big enough to draw the line and resign. The story has a better ending because they got the legal immigrants put back on. In the end it did get fixed. I think the fact that it was remedied has helped me get through it, if not over it. I didn't quit and I'm glad I didn't because I don't know if it would have made any difference. But I'm still mad about it.

Under circumstances like these, if you are going to take action, I think the best thing to do is to quit. Not stab them in the back. When do you turn on your boss in politics? Very seldom. I think it is so rare. It has to be pretty damn extreme. Before you turn on someone and start to screw 'em, YOU CAN RESIGN. You do it quietly—you leave. That's what you got to do sometimes.

Peter Edelman is an example of the right way to do it when you find your position untenable. He had a problem with a principle, he waited until it was over, and he quietly went about his life. Peter Edelman was the assistant secretary for planning and evaluation at the Department of Health and Human Services. He resigned after the passing of the welfare bill. "I resigned in protest because I disagreed profoundly with that legislation," he has said, and you've got to respect him for that.[2]

When Edelman quit, I said to myself, There's somebody with some guts. Edelman has criticized the legislation since he left the administration, which he is obviously perfectly entitled to do. But when someone is still a member of the administration, you expect something of a united front. It is usually taken as a given in any business that the executives do not criticize senior management in public.

One famous example of a cabinet member criticizing his administration's policy was David Stockman, Ronald Reagan's director of management and budget. In the course of a number of interviews, Stockman told William Greider, an editor at the *Washington Post,* about how the supply-side policies of tax cuts and money supply controls were being put together. Stockman quickly realized that Reagan couldn't keep his promise of balancing the budget if he cut taxes and refused to touch the defense budget in any meaningful way. Stockman also admitted to Greider that the economic staff didn't really understand the figures they were working with.

The policies that were being worked out were the ones that created the biggest budget deficit in the history of the entire world (with the help of President Bush). Reagan and his Milton Friedmanoids went plowing ahead no matter what people like budget director David Stockman and Marty Feldstein, chairman of the Council of Economic Advisers, said. The policy was bad. Stockman knew, Feldstein knew—anyone with a brain knew this. But Reagan kept forging on, sailing off into the red sunset. It was bad and it was dangerous. Some economists were concerned that the monetary policy and the fiscal policy that were each being pursued were so mismatched that there might be full-scale industrial collapse.

So if you're on the inside, what to do? The interesting thing about the Stockman–Greider relationship is that both of them were accused of being disloyal. Stockman spoke with Greider on condition that what he said was off the record for the *Washington Post*. So Greider wrote the notes up for a long piece in the *Atlantic*. Greider himself was attacked for not running the good stuff he had got in the *Post* ("Editor Scoops Own Paper," ran a headline). Stockman got in the news for bad-mouthing his bosses. He offered to resign, making a trip to the Oval Office that he described as being "more in the nature of a visit to the woodshed after supper." But he was kept on. He's a very principled guy, Stockman. This wasn't about sex, this was something serious. This was three trillion dollars.

The bleeding didn't stop when Reagan left. The deficit continued to rise and continued to strain the loyalties of people in government. Richard Darman, George Bush's budget director, was stuck with Bush's inane "Read my lips: No new taxes" pledge that he knew was irresponsible and practically impossible to keep. When Darman had read it before he was budget director in the draft of Bush's 1988 convention speech, he tried to get writer Peggy Noonan and adviser Roger Ailes to take it out. He kept striking it and they kept putting it back. By 1990, Bush had to make a budget deal with Congress that included tax increases. Even though he later said the deal was a mistake, he was denounced for the renunciation of the pledge.[3]

**Here's a** good example of loyalty, Republican style—send somebody a fax! After the Iowa straw poll in August 1999, when Lamar Alexander finished sixth and withdrew and Quayle finished eighth, a bunch of Quayle's aides in South Carolina quit and defected to John McCain. One of them, Edward T. McMullen, Jr., sent Dan-o a fax: "Unfortunately I have tried to reach your office this morning but have been unable to personally contact you. Your loss in Iowa and the resulting calls from your supporters forced me to conclude that South Carolina's Quayle 2000 effort is now irrevocably weakened." He handwrote on the bottom of the fax, "Your friendship and support over the years means a great deal—I hope that will continue!" Sure! Next time we're in town, Marilyn and I will be sure to look you up. Quayle's spokesman, Jonathan Baron, had to try and put a brave face on it. "The rats may be jumping off the ship but the ship's not sinking."[4]

The ship finally sank in late September when Quayle quit the race.

Now, if Bill Clinton was trying to do the same thing Reagan did, i.e., willfully ignore the needs of the country, I probably would have left him. I don't know what I would have done in those circumstances—that's a real tough road. Should you be loyal to somebody who came up with that kind of idiotic economic policy? I don't know.

Greider thinks Stockman got in so much trouble because people were not used to hearing the genuine thoughts of a top official, complete with all the doubts and fights and fudges that are involved in government. In a way, he says, they were using each other—Greider for the story, Stockman to make sure he was correctly represented when it came time to write up the record.[5]

Whatever the rights and wrongs of David Stockman's actions, Reagan didn't fire him. Now, at the risk of horrifying some of you, I'm going to concede that there are occasions when Republicans have stuck with a person. Michael Deaver was deputy White House chief of staff until he quit in May 1985. He became a lobbyist but had big legal problems in 1986 when he was charged with lying to a congressional subcommittee and a federal grand jury. He had a very close relationship with the Reagans for twenty years and they stood by him. Nancy Reagan was especially close to Deaver. As the *New York Times* commented at the time, "That the relationship continues to flourish might come as a surprise in light of Mr. Deaver's precipitous decline in influence in a city with scant sympathy for those who fall from power, if not from grace."[6]

## Robertson and Carville Agree!

I was on *Larry King* recently with Bob Woodward and Pat Robertson when a funny thing happened. Pat Robertson agreed with me. Sort of. We were talking about the idiots in Kansas who banned teaching of evolution.

Pat: "I want to ask Jim, are you saying you don't believe in a creator? You don't believe in God? Can a Democrat be an atheist?"

James (to Pat): "Let me ask you something: Do you really believe the earth is five thousand years old? Can you look in that camera and tell schoolchildren the earth is five thousand years old?"

Pat: "I believe the whole thing . . . started fifteen billion years ago but that doesn't mean I don't believe in the creator."

James: "I believe in the creator too, but we don't have to teach the earth is five thousand years old like these goofballs in Kansas."

Pat (quietly): "I don't think anybody's been doing that . . ."

James: "I'm glad we agree on that."

Pat: "Oh, Jim, you're terrific."

Larry: "Bob, why don't you investigate: How old is the earth?"

Bob: "No need to investigate: Carville and Robertson agree . . . within ten billion years."

George Bush showed himself to be a loyal guy on occasion too. If you read *All's Fair,* you'll know that he was loyal to Mary during the 1992 campaign. He stuck with people on other occasions when he might have been better off jettisoning them. In 1992, he first chose Dan Quayle as his running mate and then compounded the mistake by not dumping him during the race when it was clear he was a liability. And he kept people on like treasury secretary Nick Brady when he was president when a lot of people questioned Brady's ability.

At the beginning of his son's presidential campaign, Bush showed that he's a loyal family guy, and that that loyalty transcends a political relationship. Dan Quayle, who was running at the time, thought he could get his former boss to say a couple of words about him or agree not to attack him. "We all do what we have to do," Bush told him. So when George W.'s staff organized their first events, they made sure to hold a fundraiser in Phoenix, which is Dan Quayle's new hometown. George W. had not declared yet, so his dad represented him. He was obviously sticking with his son, not his old vice president. I bet he didn't have to think long about that.[7]

By and large, Washington isn't like the rest of the country, as we've said. If the Establishment doesn't like the president, it's clear that the American people do. In popular politics, the country shows its loyalty by voting for someone, and Bill Clinton was voted into office two times. I hope we can show a clear choice between Democratic ideals and policies and whatever passes for those in the GOP.

For me, the basic difference between a Democrat and a Republican is that a Democrat is happy. He wants to be optimistic. He says I think we can do a little better here. Whereas the Republican says human nature's rotten, everybody's rotten. I'm optimistic about America. I'm happy that we got people working; I'm happy we won the first moral war fought in history; I'm happy the crime rate's down; I'm happy the teen pregnancy rate's down; I'm happy our children are doing a little better in school. We've had a wonderful seven years under President Clinton.

Then, after that, we have to make sure that we are loyal to the legacy of President Clinton by electing a Democrat to the White House and taking every possible seat in Congress and in state and local government. Remember well that the Republicans chose to overturn the 1996 election and ignore the 1998 election. In 2000, we're not going to storm the barricades, but we're going to storm the polling places. After the first of the year we're going to organize, we're going to activate, we're going to take this country back, and we're going to take this Constitution back and these people are going to pay for what they did.

I want to say something about the Democratic presidential race. If someone were to ask me, "James, are you endorsing Al Gore out of loyalty to Bill Clinton, or because you think Al Gore would make a better president than Bill Bradley?" I would have to admit that it's a fair question. But a better question would be "Would you have endorsed Al Gore even if you *didn't* think he would make a better president than Bill Bradley?" That would be a tougher question to answer. Frankly, I don't know.

I do know that Al Gore would be as good a president as Bill Bradley. Actually, I believe deep down inside that he would be better because of the depth and breadth of his experience. This does not imply that I don't think Bradley would make a good president or that I wouldn't support him if he won the nomination or any such thing.

I think that they are both good men and each would make a good president. I would say that I'm sure the fact that President Clinton is for Mr. Gore has made me a bit more vocal than I might otherwise have been.

# I Swear:
# Loyalty Oaths,
# Hitler, and
# McCarthy

**At certain times you** are asked to publicly display your loyalty to your country by swearing an oath. The president does it at the inauguration; we all recite the Pledge of Allegiance in school. However, loyalty oaths can be abused, and they have been in our history. When they are, it shows the need for us to ask ourselves vital questions: "What am I being asked to be loyal to?" or "Why am I being asked to be loyal?" Often, when an individual has been asked to declare their loyalty to a piece of paper, they are being asked to commit themselves to something that is not deserving of loyalty. These abuses have meant that the case for loyalty has been harder to make.

An obvious example of this is Nazi Germany. In August 1934, Hitler consolidated his position by making the members of the armed forces swear an oath of allegiance to him; not to

Germany or the German constitution, which he had already trodden all over in his rise to power. The oath read:

*I swear by God this sacred oath, that I will render unconditional obe-dience to Adolf Hitler, the Fuehrer of the German Reich and people, Supreme Commander of the Armed Forces, and will be ready as a brave soldier to risk my life at any time for this oath.*

This oath meant that many Germans in the services felt that they had to carry out the Nazi leader's criminal policies because they had sworn to do so. They had not sworn an oath to Germany, whose interests they might have recognized as dif-fering from Hitler's maniacal schemes. They were only obeying orders. The historian William Shirer, who was in Germany in 1934, writes about the sense of "honor" German officers often pointed to:

*Later and often, by honoring their oath they dishonored themselves as human beings and trod in the mud the moral code of their corps.*[1]

Clearly, swearing loyalty to an individual is extremely dan-gerous because you are saying you'll follow them no matter what they do. They might turn out to be Hitler or the Rev-erend Jim Jones. This is one of those cases where you shouldn't place blind loyalty in anything above a moral code. There has to be the right motivation on both sides: the taker of the oath and the one receiving the loyalty that it demands.

## Stickin'

In contrast to the Nazi oath, our president swears loyalty to a Constitution:

*I do solemnly swear that I will faithfully execute the office of President of the United States, and will to the best of my ability, preserve, protect and defend the Constitution of the United States.*

All state and federal senators, representatives, officers, and judges also swear an oath to uphold the Constitution. Now, a large function of these oaths is ceremonial. It is part of the ritual that accompanies taking the job and marks the precise moment when it becomes official. The oath is the part of the inauguration ceremony that sticks in your mind when the president-elect holds up his hand and repeats the oath back to the chief justice. Also, by swearing to the Constitution, we were creating a difference from the British monarchy, where you swore allegiance to the king or the queen.

There can be philosophical objections to some seemingly innocuous ceremonial oaths. George Fletcher writes in his book of being asked to sign an oath swearing that he would "support" the constitutions of the United States and the State of New York before he could teach at Columbia. Firstly, how do you do that? He says, if you are a university professor, you are supposedly a champion of independent thought and freedom. So when you are asked to "faithfully discharge [your] duties," which is a part of the oath, the proper response should be to refuse to sign it.[2]

147

Fletcher also tells us about the Pledge of Allegiance. It's interesting to know that it began as an idea in a magazine, the *Youth's Companion,* to celebrate the four hundredth anniversary of Columbus's voyage. It caught on officially and in 1898 New York state was the first to require it. It's changed over time: Eisenhower added the "under God" part in 1954. The Pledge has, like the flag and the anthem, been controversial. In 1940, the Supreme Court said every schoolchild had to pledge and salute the flag, which meant that Jehovah's Witnesses could be expelled because, for them, the flag is a graven image which the Ten Commandments say you can't worship. The decision was reversed in 1943.[3] There were fights over the Pledge during Vietnam. Refusing to pledge can be a recognized protest, but no one really thinks that it shows someone is going to be disloyal to the country in any profound way.

But at certain points in our history, oaths have been used to try to actively weed out people who might be disloyal. These oaths were used on people who had not been disloyal; it was just thought that they might be at some point. George Washington used an oath to the American cause during the Revolution, and during Reconstruction some state governments made potential employees swear that they had not fought against the Union.[4]

The American right was big on loyalty oaths in the 1940s and '50s, of course. You could say they're so disloyal themselves they believe you've got to take an oath to show your loyalty. They're also saying you can reduce loyalty to a piece of paper, which is stupid. During the Cold War, they were supposed to be looking for Soviet spies. If you really are a spy, are you going to say, "Sorry, I can't take this oath because I am a spy for the Soviet Union"? Probably not.

The effort to smash communism in America, including the McCarthyism of the 1950s, was not a particularly glorious episode in our history. It is true that there were agents in this country. The release in 1995 of the "Venona" intercepts of cables from American agents to the KGB from 1943–45 proved that.[5] And Ethel and Julius Rosenberg were executed for spying. But the witch-hunts and purges and "loyalty-security programs" circumvented civil liberties and ruined the lives of innocent people. It is important that we remember the excesses of this period. For one thing, they help prove yet again that investigatory power can easily be abused.

Often at the center of events was HUAC. This began as the House Special Committee on Un-American Activities set up by Texas Democrat Martin Dies in 1938 to attack the New Deal.[6] Dies produced the first of the many lists of alleged communists. Hoover's FBI followed suit during the war. The anti-communist drive really gathered steam once the Truman Doctrine of containing the USSR was outlined in 1947 and with the outbreak of the Korean War.

The craziest anti-communist was Senator Joe McCarthy of Wisconsin. At his famous speech in Wheeling, West Virginia, in 1950, he said he had a list of 205 communists in the State Department. He didn't, but for the next four years he went on a rampage of finger-pointing and name-calling at civil servants, army officers, Adlai Stevenson, the Voice of America, and so on until a leash was put on him in 1954. McCarthy never actually caught anyone, he just went after them. (Mc-Carthy reminds me of Ken Starr in that Starr caught a couple of small players with petty crimes, but his real talent was the hunt itself—and the damage it caused.)

A couple of months after the Wheeling speech, three journalists from the *Milwaukee Journal* had lunch with him and challenged him to come up with the goods. McCarthy said:

*Listen, you bastards. I'm not going to tell you anything. I just want you to know I've got a pailful of shit, and I'm going to use it where it does me the most good.*[7]

McCarthy was the tip of the iceberg. Hoover set up the Federal Loyalty Review Board, which grilled government employees. The FBI checked up on millions of people.[8] Under a "Responsibilities Program" from 1951 to 1955, they illegally leaked information on alleged subversives to state and private authorities, who fired people as a result.[9] Private employers followed the official lead and thousands of people were thrown out of work, denied due process along the way. (Right now there are individuals who are worried about having a building called the Clinton Library in Little Rock, while the headquarters of the FBI is named after this panty-wearin' phone-tappin' file-keepin' SOB. That makes a lot of sense to me.)

As well as actual communists, whose active disloyalty to the United States was in most cases never proven, the purges caught many completely innocent liberals and non-communists too. People were driven to suicide. Many others were scared witless and didn't want to criticize anything in case someone got the wrong idea. The paranoia reached insane extremes. At one point in the mid-1950s, University of Chicago students were so afraid of putting their names on any kind of list that they wouldn't sign a petition asking to have a Coke machine in the physics lab.[10] And if you wanted a permit to fish in New York City reservoirs, you had to sign a loyalty oath.[11]

The anti-communists went to absurd lengths to establish the loyalty of the artistic community. The FBI kept files on prominent people in the arts, including six Nobel Prize–winning writers—Sinclair Lewis, Pearl S. Buck, William Faulkner, Ernest Hemingway, John Steinbeck, and Thomas Mann. A group of screenwriters and film people, the Hollywood Ten, refused to speak to HUAC and were placed on one of the notorious "blacklists." Hundreds of entertainment figures, including Zero Mostel, Pete Seeger, and Kim Hunter, couldn't get work, and in 1950 Paul Robeson was the first person to be banned from television. Howard Fast, who'd been to jail for contempt, couldn't find a publisher for his novel *Spartacus*.[12]

Artists were afraid of being too provocative. Awful, pandering B movies like *I Was a Communist for the FBI* were made. This told the true story of agent Matt Cvetic, who had infiltrated the communist party. The film poster showed the hero's girl being kidnapped by communists—"I had to sell out my own girl," read the poster. "So would you."[13] And Elia Kazan made *On the*

*Waterfront* in 1954, which showed tortured hero Marlon Brando turning in his corrupt union bosses, which was, perhaps, an attempt to say that the director's own testimony to HUAC was okay.

In the search for individuals disloyal to the country, thousands of others were asked to be disloyal to people they knew—to sell them out. There were a lot of informants. The FBI had eighty thousand informants in the war industries during the Second World War.[14] Ronald Reagan was FBI Agent T-10 when he was president of the Screen Actors Guild. It wasn't like East Germany when the Stasi files were opened and wives found that their husbands had spied on them for years for the secret police, but it was pretty bad.

In order to protect ourselves from the communists it was as though we had to become more like the communists. Like an immunization—in order to protect you from the disease, i.e., totalitarianism, you have to give yourself some of the disease, i.e., a denial of civil liberties. The way to do that is to deny more civil liberties and become more totalitarian. The witch-hunts were unfair and often unconstitutional. They used illegal methods like wiretaps and unlawful searches and they ignored due process. It's no accident that one politician who really made his name pursuing communists by whatever means was Richard M. Nixon.

This is a typical right-wing thing—to talk the talk, but never to walk the walk. In the same breath they would demand that people take a loyalty oath to the Constitution, the methods that they were using were violating the same document. They always want a speech—they always want rhetoric. The one thing that they don't ever want to do is walk the walk. They want to talk the talk; they want to give the speech.

I would also say that McCarthyism demonstrated the dangers of wildly uncontained snooping. It wasn't about loyalty, it was about politics. Throughout history, some sections of the country just love to investigate people, to accuse and pry and keep digging around even if they can't find anything very much as they go. Sometimes, when someone says they have a pailful of shit, all they have is a pailful of shit.

# The Traitors'
# Hall of Shame

**We picked four of** the great traitors: people who stabbed
an entire nation in the back by their various acts of disloyalty.

## Vidkun Quisling

The actions of the Norwegian Vidkun Quisling were so
heinous that his name has come to mean someone who turns
against their country. It's quite a feat to have a whole category
of backstabbing named after yourself. Look it up in a dictionary. Quisling took a bizarre turn after serving with great distinction in humanitarian causes in the 1920s. He started his
own fascist National Union Party in Norway in 1933. He
wanted an independent Norway fighting together with Nazi
Germany against the Soviets. So when the Germans showed
up in April 1940, he attempted to seize power on their behalf.
In February 1942, the Nazis made him minister-president of
the regime running the country. Needless to say, the Norwegian
people hated him. At the end of the war he was convicted of
treason and executed. He was hated so much, his guards

agreed among themselves to murder him if the court didn't sentence him to die.[1]

# William Joyce—"Lord Haw-Haw"

William Joyce broadcast anti-British propaganda from Germany during the Second World War. He'd say "German victory is certain" and brag about German victories. He was called "Lord Haw-Haw" because of his braying voice. On May 28, 1945, he was arrested near the Danish border. The Brits tried him for treason. Inconveniently, it turned out that Joyce was an American citizen, born in Brooklyn, and had moved to Ireland at the age of three.[2] But they hanged him anyway, allowing that he was British on a technicality, January 3, 1946. Eight Americans were indicted for broadcasting on German or Italian radio, including the poet Ezra Pound. (The British writer P. G. Wodehouse, who wrote the Jeeves and Wooster books, made some pro-German broadcasts from Paris.) Also, two Americans were arraigned for treason for their actions in the European Theater, including Lieutenant Martin James Monti, who flew his new P-38 to the German lines and said he wanted to join the Luftwaffe.[3]

# "Tokyo Rose"

Tokyo Rose was a kind of American Lord Haw-Haw. Mrs. Iva Ikuko D'Aquino, the voice of NHK Japanese Radio's English service, mocked U.S. troops in the Pacific. An American of Japanese descent, D'Aquino happened to be in Japan when the war broke out and ended up on the radio. After the war she was tried for treason and served six years in jail. D'Aquino and Mildred "Axis Sally" Gillars, who broadcast from Germany, were the first women ever accused of treason in the United States.[4]

# Benedict Arnold

Benedict Arnold (1741–1801) is the last word in treachery in this country. The name is stigmatized: How many people do you know called Benedict? The depth of hatred for Arnold must be a reflection of the heights from which he fell. Benedict Arnold was a genuine hero of the Revolution. Had he been killed any time before 1780, and it was close a number of times, he'd be right up there alongside Jefferson and Washington with the great names of American history.

Arnold had fought with distinction in an attack on Quebec in 1776 where he took a musket ball in the leg. He fought the Battle of Valcour Island, and the following year he took a leading role in stopping Burgoyne's invasion of New York. He raised the siege of Fort Stanwix and won the Battle of Bemis Heights, which was the end of the Battle of Saratoga—another decisive moment in the war. He was shot again in the same leg, which ended up two inches shorter than his other.

His troubles really began when George Washington made him military commander of Philadelphia in 1778. Arnold was crippled and practically broke—he hadn't been paid for three years or been reimbursed expenses. Philadelphia was a terrible place for him to be. A soldier who hated political interference, he was placed right where Congress had been relocated. He quickly made an enemy of radical Joseph Reed, the Calvinist head of the Supreme Executive Council of Pennsylvania, who hated Arnold's lifestyle and the fact that he wouldn't let them take revenge on Pennsylvania's Tories. Worse, Arnold courted and married Peggy Shippen, a Tory, in 1779.

The Puritans kept after Arnold and formally indicted him. A civilian committee cleared him of the charges it felt competent to judge and forwarded the two others to George Washington for a military tribunal. Reed kept going after Arnold. Peggy worked on her husband to switch sides and Arnold pleaded with Washington that his side be heard. But his wife knew a British officer from the occupation of Philadelphia, Major John André, and Arnold eventually contacted him.[5]

When he was finally court-martialed, he was found guilty of two charges of using military forces for his own private purposes. That did it for Arnold. His sentence was to be reprimanded by Washington. He was given the command of the fort at West Point. Once there, he began arranging to surrender the fort to the British. After a meeting with Arnold, Major André was captured, forcing the traitor to flee to the British. (André was quickly hanged by the Americans.)

Benedict Arnold received a total of £6,315 for his treason and was made brigadier general of the provincial troops by the British. Most of the British hated him for his treachery.

Viciously, he carried out marauding expeditions into New London, Connecticut, and Virginia. He sailed for England in December 1781 and was reunited with his family.

Arnold thought the Revolution had fatally lost its way. He had lost all perspective. He thought that by crossing over he would take thousands with him. He would reconcile the two sides. But he had the opposite effect of reinvigorating the American side, which was united in hatred of him.

How has history judged him? After he'd switched sides and was raiding into Virginia, he is supposed to have asked someone what they thought would happen to him if he were captured.

*"They will cut off that leg of yours wounded at Quebec and Saratoga, and bury it with all the honors of war, and then hang the rest of you on a gibbet."*[6]

# The Sports Section:
# Jackie Robinson,
# Pee Wee Reese,
# and Loyalty in
# Sports

**Sports is like the** army in that you show your loyalty by wearing a uniform. Players obviously wear them so you can see who to pass to, and fans buy $150 replicas to show that they are loyal followers. Sports also drafts people, but you don't get shot at in the NBA and you can't make $8 million a year in the U.S. Navy, so enough of the bogus military analogies. But emotions run so high among sports fans that you'd think the future of the country was at stake every time their team took the field. Pro sports does reflect what's going on in society and in some cases has been a force for good. As in everything else, there are good people and bad people, loyalty and disloyalty, and some great examples of guys sticking with other guys and with their teams that we should look at.

Jackie Robinson is one of the great all-time American heroes. In 1947, Robinson broke Jim Crow in baseball when he became the first black man to play in the major leagues in the twentieth century. He went on to be a great player, a Hall of Famer, and he remains a compelling role model for millions of Americans. Jackie Robinson's achievements owe everything to the man's formidable strength and matchless integrity. But our book is more about loyalty than courage, and I want to focus on a public act by Pee Wee Reese, a teammate of Robinson's, that strikes me as a great example of a loyal act of lasting significance.

We already know Jackie Robinson was a loyal guy—loyal to his wife, Rachel, his team, and his race. When Robinson was in the Army in 1943, he was court-martialed after an incident when a white bus driver tried to get him to sit at the back in the segregated section.[1]

Rachel Robinson is a wonderful person. I know her, having met her through my good friend Len Coleman, who was until recently president of the National League. She asked me to call her Rachel one time and I said, "I'm sorry, I just can't do it, Mrs. Robinson."

Jackie Robinson was brought to the major leagues by Branch Rickey, part-owner and general manager of the Dodgers. Rickey was a devout Christian who wouldn't go to games on a Sunday. He'd been around baseball a long time. In 1904, he'd been manager of the Ohio Wesleyan team that went to South Bend to play Notre Dame. His team had one black player, Charles Thomas. When the team went to their hotel, Thomas wasn't let in, but Rickey insisted that Thomas be allowed to share his room. Rickey later found Thomas trying to peel the flesh off his hands, saying, "Damned skin . . . damned skin." Rickey vowed to do something about segregation in baseball. A portrait of Lincoln hung in his office.[2] In our gallery of loyal people in this story, Rickey stuck with his vision of integrated baseball.

Robinson started out in the Dodger organization as a shortstop. The Dodger shortstop, before Robinson was called up, was a guy from Kentucky, Harold Henry "Pee Wee" Reese. When Reese found out about the signing of Robinson, according to Roger Kahn's great book about the Dodgers, *The Boys of Summer*, he was on his way back from Guam and his naval duty in the war. He thought about what it would be like if he, Reese, went to play in the Negro Leagues and decided that if Robinson beat him out at short, then he'd deserve it.[3] (In the end, Robinson moved to second base.)

Not everyone was so accommodating. As Robinson neared the major league club, a group of Southern Dodgers like Eddie Stanky and Dixie Walker talked about getting up a petition saying they wouldn't play with a black man. Leo Durocher, the Dodgers' manager, said, "Well, boys, you know what you can do with that petition. You can wipe your ass with it."[4] Robinson signed with the big club at the start of the 1947 season for the league minimum salary, $5,000.

Before he signed Robinson, Branch Rickey had rehearsed for him all the terrible slurs he'd face. Right away, Robinson had to put up with all that Rickey had warned him about and more. He was way out there, on his own, a pioneer. Arnold Rampersad chronicles Robinson's season in his biography. He reports that Jimmy Cannon of the *New York Post* said Jackie Robinson was "the loneliest man I have ever seen in sports." And in a game with the Phillies on April 27, the opposition's Alabama-born manager, Ben Chapman, led a torrent of disgusting racist abuse from the dugout. According to Jackie, "It brought me nearer to cracking up than I ever had been." But Robinson's teammates, including Stanky and Walker this time, stood up for him and shouted back. Robinson, who wanted to go over and stick one on someone, kept a promise he made to Rickey to turn the other cheek for three years, and scored the only run in a 1–0 win.[5]

Robinson continued to take abuse—there were other stories of players' strikes and by the end of May he'd been hit by pitches as often as anyone in the whole of the previous season. But he'd survived and won. In a game with the Pirates, Robinson had an almighty collision with Pittsburgh first baseman Hank Greenberg. "Stick in there. You're doing fine," Greenberg said. Greenberg knew what he was talking about. He had been abused by bigots for years because he was Jewish.

All the while, Pee Wee Reese went about his job. He was the universally respected captain of the team. By his example, he worked to keep the team together and working for the same goal. Roger Kahn describes Reese's attitude toward Robinson:

*He was Jackie Robinson's friend. They played hit-and-run together and cards and horses. Anyone who resented Robinson for his color or—more common—for the combination of color and aggressiveness found himself contending not only with Jack, but with the captain. Aware, but unselfconscious, Reese and Robinson came to personify integration. If a man didn't like what they personified, why, he had better not play for the Dodgers.*[6]

In one game, Reese made a gesture that stands to this day as one of the great public displays of loyalty. Pee Wee Reese was clearly a good man who did a good thing. There is disagreement as to where the incident took place. Some people say it was in Cincinnati, some people say it was in Boston. It doesn't matter. Both are fine American cities, neither of which is particularly known for its enlightened racial views. (But even they are cities, I might say, that have a better racial history than Baton Rouge.)

Disgusted by the virulent bigoted garbage being shouted at Robinson, Reese made a point of standing next to his second baseman on the field and putting his arm around Jackie Robinson's shoulder. It was a quiet thing, but the symbolism was and is obvious and powerful. At a difficult and troubled time, these two men stood for something much more than a double-play combination on a baseball team.

Pee Wee Reese died on August 14, 1999. At his funeral in Louisville, Reese's contribution to Jackie Robinson's season and the cause of integration were remembered. Rachel Robinson said, "Jack and I always felt like Pee Wee was somebody you could trust and believe in. . . . Pee Wee was more than a friend. He was a good man."[7] An old colleague of Reese's, Joe Black, traveled to Louisville for the funeral. He was one of the first African-Americans to follow Jackie Robinson into the league. At the funeral, he said:

*When Pee Wee Reese reached out to Jackie, all of us in the Negro Leagues smiled and said it was the first time a white guy had accepted us. When I finally got up to Brooklyn, I went up to Pee Wee and said, "Black people love you. When you touched Jackie, you touched all of us." With Pee Wee, it was No. 1 on his uniform and No. 1 in our hearts.*[8]

And today, Peter Golenbock's kids' book about the two of them, *Teammates,* is used to teach racial harmony to elementary school children.

Now, I was in college when James Meredith started at Ole Miss. I went to segregated schools. I wish I had been as strong a person as Pee Wee Reese.

He was loyal to a teammate. What was Pee Wee Reese thinking about? Was he thinking about being loyal to the Dodgers or being loyal to Robinson? Did he do it for his teammate, or did he do it for his team? He may have acted for any combination of reasons. We don't know. If you had asked him, he might or might not have been able to give an eloquent dissertation about the fundamental rights of men. He did say this later:

*I wasn't trying to think of myself as being the Great White Father. It didn't matter to me whether he was black or green, he had a right to be there, too.*[9]

166

**People do** love their teams. Me, I root for my college teams the most. Teams are like friends: They need you when the going is bad. I mean it's easy to be a Yankee fan. Even when they're bad, like they were in the 1980s, you know you can just stick around a while and they'll be good again. A real fan is a Red Sox fan. Even when the Red Sox are good you know they'll screw it up. Or fate will intervene. Or a combination (like blown calls plus three hundred errors in the 1999 ALCS). Same with the Cubs.

Another real fan is an Expos fan who still shows up. Expos fans face the ultimate shaft: the team getting moved. When guys like Robert Irsay move the Baltimore Colts to Indianapolis in the middle of the night, they make a special place for themselves in local infamy. Now, when a guy like Art Modell runs out on Cleveland, he's being disloyal to them, but he fills the void in Baltimore. Just don't show up at the Rock and Roll Hall of Fame anytime soon, Art.

The owner who suffered the most abuse was Walter O'Malley, who took the beloved Dodgers out of Brooklyn. There's a story about the newspaper writers and Brooklyn fans Jack Newfield and Pete Hamill sitting in a bar years later talking about writing a piece on "The Ten Worst Human Beings Who Ever Lived."[10] They each wrote their top three on a napkin and compared notes. They'd both written the same thing:

1. Hitler
2. Stalin
3. Walter O'Malley

## Dean Smith

Dean Smith is a loyal guy who happens to work in sports. He stuck as head coach of the University of North Carolina for thirty-six years and 1,133 games. In his autobiography Smith talks about "The Carolina Way" that brought him great success.[11] He describes a tremendous amount of dedication and hard work. It wasn't easy—in 1964 things were going so bad, Smith was hung in effigy on the campus. But from 1971, UNC averaged twenty-seven wins a season for twenty-seven seasons and won two National Championships along the way. But he's not just loyal to his school. The book shows that his first thought is to stick with his guys.

First, Dean Smith writes about the great influence of his father, Alfred, also a coach, who taught Dean, among other things, to value everybody the same. In 1934, Alfred picked Paul Terry, the son of a janitor at the local bank, to play on his Emporia High School, Emporia, Kansas, basketball team. Paul Terry is black, and he integrated high school sports in Kansas. Dean Smith hates racism. In 1989, J. R. Reid was on the team. He is black. Duke fans held up a sign that said, "J. R. Can't Reid." Smith thought it was a racial slur and said at a press conference that Reid and another black player, Scott Williams, had better combined SATs than two white Duke players, Danny Ferry and Christian Laettner. Talk about sticking it to them.

He teaches his players to play unselfishly, to play hard, smart, and together. He started the practice of a player who's scored pointing to the guy who's given him the assist. Drawn together by their common purpose, coach and players and staff become like one huge extended family. He's loyal to them, they're loyal to him, and they're all loyal to each other. One player, Jeff Lebo, class of '89, now a coach, said:

> *It's a fraternity. I might not know a guy who played for Coach Smith in 1976, but I know if I needed help and picked up the phone and called that guy, he'd be there for me. That's what a lot of people don't understand. The group would run to help anybody.*[12]

George Karl, class of 1973 and the coach of the Milwaukee Bucks, says, "We get a lot of ribbing from the other players and colleges, but we're pretty loyal."[13] Black and white, they're in each other's weddings, staying in touch, keeping the connectors going.

When Dean Smith's players were getting all this money to play in the NBA he supported them, he didn't resist it. He doesn't stand in a guy's way. If he thinks a player can go top five in the draft and set himself up for life with one contract, he thinks he should go. He didn't try to talk James Worthy into coming back in 1982 and helped him make his decision. He was ecstatic when the Lakers picked him number one, and the guy was leaving the program! When Michael Jordan decided to go pro, Smith helped him negotiate his contract. He wants what's best for the young man, not for Dean Smith or the school. Almost all the guys who leave UNC early complete their degrees anyway.

But Dean Smith remembers all his players, not just the fifty-two who played in the NBA or ABA. He knows what all his players have done with their lives because he's interested in the whole man, not just the student. He is a guy who recognized changes in the game and adapted, always staying loyal to the young men in his charge. Not everybody in sports is some over-paid blabbermouth. I love Dean Smith.

What I think Pee Wee was doing was saying, "I'm the shortstop, this guy's the second baseman. He's my teammate and I'm the captain." It was a visceral and even purer sense of loyalty than anything too long considered. Again, we say that if it's something you have to think about too much, it's not so much an act of loyalty, it's calculated.

In the end, it doesn't really matter why he did it. He had clearly wrestled with the question. Once you have wrestled with a question like that, there's no guarantee that you come out on the right side. He ended up on the right side, even if we don't know precisely why. Whatever he was thinking, he put his arm around his shoulder. He was certainly loyal to something. It was a loyalty that took great courage. Would he have agreed with *Brown v. Board of Education of Topeka*? But he acted in 1947, before any of this came about. He did what he did, and that's what counts. He did a fine thing.

**The 1999** baseball season saw three players head toward the elite 3,000-hit club. Cal Ripken, Jr., has received a huge amount of acclaim for what he has done with the Baltimore Orioles and rightly so. Sadly for Cal, his season ended on September 22 through injury when he was nine hits shy of the landmark. Two players did reach the plateau, and in the same week: Wade Boggs and Tony Gwynn.

I want to say something about Tony Gwynn. He's stuck with the San Diego Padres his whole career, even when they dumped all their good players except for him a couple of years ago. Even when he could have gotten a whole lot more money and publicity and endorsements somewhere else. This guy is the best hitter of his generation and he was loyal to a team that often didn't seem interested in winning. He could have DH'd in the American League and got a lot more cheap hits. (Hit number 3,006 was important to Tony because that meant he'd gotten 3,000 as a position player in the National League. He's had six hits as a DH in interleague play.)

He was delighted to get number 3,000 on his mom, Vendella's, sixty-fourth birthday. "My parents raised me right," he said afterward. "I owe a lot to my mom and dad. Having my mom here is a special thing for me, because my mom and dad played a special part in my life."[14]

He spoke about how his dad had tried to persuade him to leave San Diego in 1993. Before Tony could explain why it was so important for him to stay, his dad died.

*He would understand now. Being in San Diego is where I'm supposed to be. Here I am, still here. So to do this in a Padres uniform, being in the National League for my whole career, this really means a lot to me.*[15]

And on the night he got his 3,000th hit in Montreal, he went four-for-five.

# The Business Section: Brand Loyalty and Spending Money

**When it comes to** spending money, many people are creatures of habit. We vest ourselves in a commercial product like we identify with a team. My brother-in-law would not let any beer other than a Budweiser touch his lips. All told, people pay billions of dollars in premiums to buy a particular brand, because the brand name usually isn't the cheapest. These are people who'll buy Planters peanuts as opposed to anyone else's peanuts. Or Timberland boots rather than another line of boots.

And for the businesses themselves, loyalty is a commodity that companies trade on. They spend billions of dollars to make their brand the biggest—Tide, Coke, Nike, Levi's. Some brands are so big, they are the product: Xerox, Kleenex, Rollerblade. So why are people loyal to brands, and when will they use considerations other than the name on the label?

If you go to a library or bookstore and look into this a little bit, you'll find a lot of books about marketing that discuss concepts like "brand equity." They are supposed to explain why somebody will spend $150 for a pair of Nikes. They're buying into the image of performance.[1] I guess people do think that if they wear Nike they'll be able to drain a jumper like Michael Jordan or hit a golf ball like Tiger Woods.

Some of these concepts apply in the work I do with politicians. Some people get upset when politicians are talked about like any other product, but it's clear that there are parallels. You work to establish a candidate and have him or her associated with certain key concepts. You do that by refining the message and getting the message out there. That's wholesale politics. And you get them to do retail politics by meeting people, shaking hands, saying hello. That helps build trust. So it's a lot like companies and their brands. You have to hope you're working with a Cadillac, not an Edsel.

There are particular companies whose brands are held up in the literature as great success stories. They have been able to win customers' loyalty and keep it. Like Saturn cars. And Procter & Gamble has had a lot of success stories.[2] Since the 1930s P&G has aggressively managed its brands. Now it has three hundred: Tide, Dawn, Crisco, Crest, Scope, Bounce, Head & Shoulders, Pepto-Bismol, and so on.

How do companies like P&G succeed? They spend money in developing products and they innovate. They are big on customer service. They give you 800 numbers for suggestions and tips and they follow up on complaints. They work to establish a consumer's confidence in the product. And they advertise. A lot. P&G spends $3 billion a year on advertising. TV, radio, print, billboards, posters. Banners behind airplanes.

Advertising is key. Companies spend fortunes coming up with campaigns and slogans and they pay people good money to appear in their slots. Absolut vodka had a great campaign that continues all over the country today. Using it, they went from five thousand cases of vodka a year to 2.5 million cases a year and the number one import brand position by the late 1980s.[3] The image given by the advertising is vital because, when you come down to it, regular vodka's just vodka. (And they weren't selling any of this to me: I'm a gin man myself.)

Now you will understand why I am particularly concerned about hair care and the various shampoos, conditioners, oils, and the like that people apparently use. I wish I could develop a loyalty to somebody's shampoo at this point. I asked someone I know who works at Clairol about successful shampoos. She told me it's all about the advertising. Clairol came out with an Herbal Essences shampoo that was doing okay but they relaunched it with a new advertising campaign. "A totally organic experience" was the catchphrase. This brand went through the roof and it's now number two in the category. They didn't change the formulation or anything. Now it's a "mega-brand" with a line of body washes and facial care products.[4] And shampoo's like vodka—it's all pretty much the same gunk.

The essential thing to get brand loyalty is that the stuff you put out has to be good and proved to be good over a long period. When people are comfortable with something and they trust it, they'll pay more for it because they think they're getting good value, even if the stuff is more expensive. Sticking with the hair examples, P&G sells half the shampoo in China, even though it's three times the cost of the local stuff.[5]

We're loyal brand people in my house. My wife will not let me buy any old ibuprofen; she insists that I buy Advil. I say it's the same thing and she just says it doesn't work as well. But it is literally the same stuff. You look at the active ingredients, it is precisely the same. That's not a lifestyle decision. (If you ask me, Alka-Seltzer works better than anything else.) And I am a sucker for packaging, I don't know why. I'll buy the thing with the prettiest bow on it.

Companies will go to great lengths to secure your loyalty. Airlines. Of any product that I consume, the one I consume the most is airplane travel. You become so vested in the frequent flyer thing. People will go to a great inconvenience to stay with one airline. I belong to all of the frequent flyer clubs and they seemed like a good idea when they came out and people got obsessed by them. They are designed to get your loyalty. You become a One-K-Executive-Platinum-Dividend-Silver-Bullet member and it makes you put up with inane crap you would not normally put up with. The last time we counted, I think we had a million and a half of these miles. Frankly, I would give them all back if they would give me something decent to eat, or give me a little more leg room, or get my bags back to me in good time. After you travel a gazillion miles, the last thing you want to do is fly somewhere.

There is a limit to brand loyalty. People find that their greater loyalty is to their wallet. Some people will always buy the generic. In the late 1980s, P&G found that their brands

**Back after** this: There is an old German proverb: "Whose bread I eat, his song I sing." In our house, there are some brands whose praises we sing especially loudly. We are very loyal to:
American Express
Alka-Seltzer
Cotton
ESPN
Heineken
Little Debbie Snack Cakes
Nike (I have done some work for Reebok too. Don't tell.)
And anyone else whose commercials Mary or I might appear in.

weren't growing as fast as they were accustomed to. Part of it was that the products were too expensive. Their best consumers were paying about $725 a year more for their products than the generic equivalent. So they cut prices.[6] This shows that, by and large, the average consumer is smart about how they spend their money. They'll spend money on good products that are familiar to them as long as the price isn't inflated. Various factors come into play when someone is spending money. This is even more the case with things that have a service element attached to them. That is, when there are people involved. There's a big difference between being loyal to a brand of toothpaste and a restaurant.

A friend of mine said to me: You go to New York a lot, what's the best hotel up there? My answer is it's the one that they know you at. If they don't know you, you can't get in. Or if you can get in, you're going to get a bad room. And if you get in and get a bad room and you don't know them, you don't know who to complain to. If you say which has the best building or the prettiest lobby, that's one thing. But where loyalty really counts in this kind of decision is when you go again and again and you build up relationships.

For hotels, I have a relationship with a woman named Ellie Peters. She's worked at a bunch of hotels, the latest being the Essex House, so I moved to the Essex House after she did. I don't care about the edifice, I care that Ellie Peters is there so if I'm called up to New York on business and I need a room, I can get one. Also, I am loyal to running every day and one of the five best runs in America is out of my front door right there in Central Park. There might be better hotels than the Essex House but they're not better for me. I'm not loyal to the Westin brand or any such thing, I'm loyal to Ellie Peters. So, for me, when you're talking about service, life is not just the pursuit of finding the best, or even the cheapest or the best value, life is the pursuit of finding what works the best for you.

The same goes with me for restaurants. A lot of people tease me because I eat at the Palm in Washington a lot. The owner, Tommy Jacamo, is my friend. If I call Tommy and say, "I need a table," I can get one. My family came up to see me some years ago and they stopped off in Washington and I sent them to the Palm to get supper. I called in to see how it was going and they reported everything was fine except that Thomas wanted fried shrimp and they said they didn't have it on the

**There's another** restaurant I have to mention. It would be stupid not to, not to say disloyal. That's because it's my restaurant—mine with Mary and Todd De Lorenzo, who runs everything for us. When I think of loyal employees, I think of Todd first—I dedicated my last book to him. The restaurant will be in Washington, D.C., and it's called Emerson's, named after, you guessed it, our younger daughter. Emerson's will open around April 2000 at 1250 24th Street (24th and M), serving a mix of Northern and Southern American cuisine. You can bet Mary, Todd, and I will be extremely loyal to Emerson's.

menu at night, they only had it at lunch. I said, "Get Tommy on the phone." I said to Tommy, "Goddamn it, get somebody in the kitchen and fix the boy some fried shrimp. How can you have it at noon and not at night?" He did it. My nephew was forever impressed that I got him his fried shrimp. If I went to some fancy-ass restaurant, I couldn't do that.

When I go to New York, I eat at the Gramercy Tavern or the Union Square Café or Eleven Madison, one of the places that Danny Meyer owns and Richard Coraine manages. They have great food and Danny and Richard are my dear friends. All of life is not just a rush to find the best or the cheapest thing. Sometimes you find people you have relationships with that make the experience that much better. I've done this through my life. When I was in Baton Rouge, I went to George's Bar. I now have the extreme good fortune to be able to go to these places in New York (or go with someone who can pick up the tab). We all have a part of us that wants to find a place where we feel we belong.

I understand why people go on the Internet to find the cheapest flight or why they go out of their way to get the best deal on a car. I understand the desire to save money. But over a period of time, I believe that the loss of real human contact affects people. I do worry that my children are growing up in a world where every decision is being made on the basis of efficiency. We are removing a lot of the human element.

Personally, I would rather go to breakfast and be served by someone who is nice and asks me about the kids but who might bring me scrambled eggs when I ordered them fried than go to some wonderfully efficient place that got everything right but where they don't give a damn about you as a human being. The quality of the food isn't everything. I remember reading about a guy in Ohio who went to a restaurant every day for lunch and dinner and a waitress there looked after him really well. He left her a fortune. There might well have been better places to eat in that town, but I bet he went there because of the warmth of the human contact.

I'm like my father when it comes to sticking with places. On the few occasions the family went to New Orleans, the only place we ever ate in was Arnaud's restaurant. My father was absolutely convinced that Arnaud's was the best restaurant in New Orleans. There was a certain waiter there, Mr. Horry, who waited on us and looked after us. It didn't matter whether Arnaud's really was the best restaurant in New Orleans, or if it was even a good restaurant. My Daddy felt comfortable there and so we ate at Arnaud's. Mary and I got married in New Orleans, so guess where we had our reception?

I remember a time when I got really steamed up about a commercial product. My Daddy's store in Carville used to sell Texaco gas. As a kid, I used to be very impressed with the fact that Texaco was in all forty-eight states (this was before there were fifty). Louisiana was a large producer of petroleum and I had two cousins whose fathers worked for oil companies: Jack, whose daddy worked for Shell, and Fritz, whose daddy worked for Esso (this was way back before Exxon was created).

We three boys would have intense fights about which was the best gasoline. I would get all excited and say that Texaco was the best. Jack was firmly convinced Shell was the best and Fritz, for his part, was equally sure that Esso had no equal.

Anyway, one day we were in the midst of this discussion and my uncle who worked for Esso heard the commotion and walked into the room. He said, "What are you boys arguing about?" We said it was about who made the best gas and he laughed and said, "Well you boys are not arguing about very much. It's all the same stuff. If you run a little short, we sell you some under the fence. If we run a little short, you sell us some. We just pass it back and forth."

Well, I was completely devastated. I felt I'd been had by somebody. I'd been arguing with my cousins all this time and we come to find out it's all the same stuff. We cousins stopped arguing. Eventually my father switched to Esso anyway because his brother worked there. And now, when I need gas, I stop at the first gas station I see.

# The Arts Section: Shakespeare, *The Sopranos,* and Andy Griffith

**Just about every decent** dramatic book, movie, or play is going to have a theme of conflicted loyalty in it at some point. Loyalty, or, rather, disloyalty, is the very essence of drama. It makes a story. I mean, take all the stories in the Bible. Everyone who gets in trouble has been disloyal to God. Look at Adam and Eve. When the Deluge came and Noah and his family were saved, there was a very strong message. The entire world was in such terrible moral shape that they were all rubbed out. Be loyal to God. (Of course, if we lived in Kansas, this story is not a story, it is news, as it was literally true. It took place three weeks ago last Thursday, just before *Star Wars Episode I* opened.) So take apart any great story, and there's loyalty at its heart.

*Romeo and Juliet.* The lovers are lovers despite the fact that their families are feuding and hate each other. Their loyalty is to each other and not their family. This doesn't do them much good, because, as anyone who's seen *Shakespeare in Love* can tell you, Leonardo DiCaprio and Claire Danes both die in the end (or is that some other movie?). Shakespeare has the best disloyal characters, if you know what I mean.

The world champion backstabber, literally, is Brutus in *Julius Caesar.* Brutus is Caesar's closest adviser and confidant. When Caesar is stabbed by his enemies and he sees that Brutus is among them he says, "Et tu, Brute," i.e., "And you too, you disloyal bastard?" Shakespeare is sure to have the conspirators pay for their disloyalty by pitting them against the great political operator and loyal guy, Mark Antony. He makes the famous "Friends, Romans, countrymen" speech that wins over the crowd and Brutus ends up running on his own sword. Often in Shakespeare people choose a noble death hoping that it will let them off all the terrible things they have done in their lives. It ain't that easy in politics these days.

One of the reasons Shakespeare is the greatest writer of all is that he covers absolutely everything somewhere in one of his plays. Every conceivable moral dilemma or family feud or emotional problem, he's attended to it somewhere. Shakespeare and Dante, whose work I have read a very little of. If William Bennett wants to talk about violence on TV and the like, why doesn't he mention what goes on in Dante's *Inferno*? (I'm joking.) Anyway, Dante maps out the circles of hell and precisely which sinners occupy the places there. In the Eighth Circle, by which point conditions are pretty bad, he has, beneath Flatterers, Horned Devils with Lashes, Fortune-tellers, and Diviners, and just above Thieves—Hypocrites. When you

**If we** had a travel section in this book, we'd mention this interesting-looking place there. But we don't have a travel section, so it has to go here. Where does the loyal family go on holiday? The Loyalty Islands of course. The Loyalty Islands are Ouvéa, Lifou, and Maré. They are situated, as if you needed me to tell you, in the South Pacific, east of Australia. They're part of New Caledonia, which is an overseas territory of France. Beautiful white sand beaches and peaceful shaded lagoons await the intrepid traveler to the Loyalty Islands. There is some question as to the current loyalty of the Loyalty Islands, as sections of the population of New Caledonia want to cut their links to France. Perhaps we should club together, buy some land, and build a retirement home there for tired old Republican congressmen, worn out after years of watching their backs.

recall our discussion of hypocrites, take a look at the *Inferno* and figure out which of them should get which punishment.

The fictional family that pays the most attention to sticking is The Family—the Mafia. Of course we can see that the loyalty of the members of the Corleone clan is completely overdeveloped. I guess the most striking example in the movies is in *The Godfather, Part II* when Michael (Al Pacino) has his brother, poor old Fredo (John Cazale), taken out and shot in the rowboat after a spot of fishing. Fredo was disloyal, but he was also really stupid. Nobody ever gets reprimanded in the *Godfather* movies, they just get shot. Or they are ever so subtly encouraged to kill themselves.

People seem to love this stuff. There have been more mob families in the movies than there ever were in the real world. The new Family is *The Sopranos,* a show that I like myself. David Chase, the creator, when asked why people like these stories, was quoted as saying, "It has to do with loyalty, high-stakes living. And people identify oddly enough with the family."[1] Which is strange if you think about it. But I guess someone's sitting at home watching an informer get strangled with a length of phone wire thinking, "Yeah, Uncle Jimmy was a bit like that."

I must admit there's more chance of my watching *The Sopranos* than reading Dante at this point. But my all-time favorite television program has to be *The Andy Griffith Show.* Like Shakespeare and Dante, there's everything here. Andy and Barney. Barney works for Andy but they're more like friends. Very loyal to each other. I especially remember one show that discussed loyalty in an inventive way.

It goes something like this. Andy shows up at some very powerful guy's office to arrest him. He's a local newspaper baron, a kind of Rupert Murdoch figure. I think he's got a bunch of unpaid parking tickets outstanding or something. The baron says to Andy, "I'm going to crush you," and he gets this reporter to interview Barney about Andy. Now Barney's pretty dumb and the reporter is attractive and she gets Barney to say some stuff about Andy, about how he's kind of lax—he uses a squad car to deliver groceries and he doesn't even carry a gun. But Barney is being stupid rather than disloyal.

**There's a** good example of someone deciding his loyalties in the heat of the moment in Alexandre Dumas's great adventure novel *The Three Musketeers*. D'Artagnan is a country boy who comes to Paris determined to become a musketeer, one of the King's bodyguard who are in permanent conflict with the evil Cardinal's soldiers. He tries to introduce himself to the musketeers but only succeeds in insulting Athos, Porthos, and Aramis, the three heroes of the novel's title. The way insults are settled is with a duel, so D'Artagnan is faced with fights with each of the three musketeers, one after another. But duels are banned and one way the Cardinal gets at the King's men is to catch them fighting. So right as they are about to begin the first duel, they are set upon by the Cardinal's men:

> At this moment, d'Artagnan made a swift decision. It was one of those occasions which determines a man's whole future for better or worse. D'Artagnan had to choose between the King and the Cardinal and, the choice once made, to abide by it. To fight was to disobey the law, and that meant risking his head, in other words, making a life-long enemy of a minister who was more powerful than the King himself. Our hero realized all this in a flash and yet, to his credit be it said, he did not hesitate for a moment. He turned to the musketeers and cried: "Gentlemen, I think there's some mistake. Monsieur Athos said there were only three of us. I make it four."[2]

D'Artagnan went with his gut and acted on his instinct. He's clearly our kind of guy, if not a very good Catholic boy.

The reporter gets what she wants and the paper runs this article about Andy and the authorities unleash Ken Starr on him. I think they spent about fifty dollars on the investigation, not fifty million. But Andy is suspended and there's going to be a hearing and they call Barney. The judge calls up Barney and they've kind of got him. The judge says, "Did you say this?" and "Did you say that?" and he has to say, "Yes." The judge says, "That's all, you can step down." But Barney asks if he can say something and the judge lets him and he presents this eloquent defense of Andy. Barney knows he's screwed up but he stands up and tells everyone what a good guy he is and how he does a great job for the community and everything and there's nothing else for it and the judge lets him off. I love that show.

It's harder for me to say what my favorite book is. It's a real toss-up. I love *To Kill a Mockingbird*, but as we are talking about loyalty, I should give a nod to *All the King's Men* by Robert Penn Warren. It is such a rich and wonderful book, I've probably read it five times. It has fantastic stuff about politics and politicians and how often loyalties are totally skewed. Jack was compromised in there. I doubt that there's anybody that's served a king that hasn't felt compromised from time to time. I think the message is: If you don't want to be compromised, be the king.

# Louisiana
# Loyalty Lunch

**In Louisiana, the two** great preoccupations and pillars of society are food and the family. We have an expression for great food. Now you love your family very much, but when food is good, when it's indescribably good, you get overcome. When this food is involved and it's a conflict between the food and your family, well, for once, your family loses. So you say it's good enough to make you slap your grandmother. The indescribable would make you do the unthinkable.

Centered around Slap Your Grandma Oyster Loaf, these recipes make a Louisiana loyalty lunch (or dinner or supper).

### Slap Your Grandma Oyster Loaf

One to two dozen oysters
About ⅓ cup each of cornmeal, corn flour, and all-purpose flour
About 1 tablespoon of Chef Paul Prudhomme's Seafood Magic seasoning*
Enough lard for frying

*We've adapted Chef Paul's recipe for fried oysters. Our thanks to him: the best chef in the South and a truly loyal Louisianan.

189

One loaf of white bread, unsliced
One stick of butter (adjust for taste)

1. At least 1 hour before serving: Ice beer down. You should do steps 1 through 4 of the french fries recipe too. (See below.)
2. Preheat oven to 350° F.
3. Take the oysters—plump oysters, the plumpest you can find. Drain them. Mix together the cornmeal, corn flour, and all-purpose flour with Chef Paul's seasoning.
4. Toss the oysters in the seasoned cornmeal mix to coat them.
5. Use a deep fryer or large saucepan. Drop the oysters in lard—not canola, not sunflower oil nor any of that other bullshit (Chef Paul's recipe does use vegetable oil). Peanut oil cut with lard, if you must, or just pure lard. Because this is not a health-conscious recipe. You are not going to slap your grandmother over a carrot stick or a piece of tofu. Fry the oysters in a single layer until crisp and brown—1 to 1½ minutes. Make sure the oil is good and hot—the oil should be 375°.
6. Take a whole loaf of unsliced white bread, not whole wheat multigrain rubbish, not oat bread. Cut the top off and hollow out the insides, leaving about an inch around for support.
7. Melt butter. Not margarine or Olestra or any of that other crap. Take a mop and mop the inside of the bread. As even as you can get it.
8. Put the bread in an oven until it gets slightly toasty. Take it out. Dump oysters in.

9. Serve with cocktail sauce and tartar sauce. The trick with
   any fried food is to serve it as quickly after you've made it as
   possible. It has a shelf life of about five seconds.
   *For 4 people, you need at least 2 loaves.*

## Tartar Sauce

Buy good mayonnaise or make your own. I like to do that and
it tastes a lot better.
   Chop finely: sweet pickles, olives, green onions.
   Add a couple of dashes of Tabasco sauce.
   *Mix and serve.*

## Cocktail Sauce

Take ketchup, lemon juice, a little horseradish, Lea & Perrins,
Tabasco.
   Don't ask me how much of each.
   Just kind of eyeball it but don't overwhelm with horseradish.
   *Mix and serve.*

## French Fries

Two pounds russet potatoes
Oil for deep frying
Salt (to taste)
One brown paper bag

1. Take the russet potatoes. Don't worry if they sit around the
   kitchen a couple of weeks. The older the better, within reason. There's some chemical reason to do with starch that

191

makes older potatoes fry better. I don't recall exactly what the reason is; just trust me. Peel 'em. (You can leave the skins on, if you prefer.)

2. Get a big bowl of iced water ready.
3. Use a good knife. If you've got a Mandoline slicer and know how to use one, then go ahead, but I've never figured out how to do it without cutting myself. Cut potatoes into quarter-inch strips (lengthwise).
4. Put 'em in the iced water for at least 1 hour, up to 36 hours. I saw a recipe in the *New York Times* that said 48 hours, but this is impulse food, Mr. Sulzberger.
5. Get oil up to 325 degrees. A good product is the DeLonghi Roto Fryer. Use that if you have one. Use peanut oil and add a couple of dollops of bacon grease for texture. Three or four tablespoons. If your cholesterol is under 150, use a lot. Over 150, 1 tablespoon. Check with your internist. (I've done the fries in olive oil and never had a problem.)
6. Fry them at 325 for about 10 minutes until they just turn golden. Do this ahead of time. Put the fries aside.
7. Five minutes before you get ready to eat, finish them off at 370.
8. Take a brown paper bag. Never use paper towels. Only idiots use paper towels. Put fries in the bag. Consistent with your blood pressure, add adequate but not too much salt. Shake 'em up real good.
9. Serve. Have some ketchup handy. I like a little ketchup. I am a believer in cold ketchup. Some like it at room temperature. *Serves 4*

# Stickin'

## Cole Slaw

One head of cabbage
Selection of vegetables
White wine vinegar
Extra-virgin olive oil
Lea & Perrins sauce
Sugar
Salt and fresh-ground pepper
(All to taste)

1. Shred the head of cabbage the best way you can. I use a 12-inch chef's knife. You can use a food processor.
2. Add any combination of the following (chopped):
   Green onions,
   Carrots,
   Vidalia onions,
   Olives stuffed with pimento,
   Any other reasonable vegetable.
3. Take a decent quality white wine vinegar. Shake some on. Add a good bit of good-quality olive oil—I like a ratio of 6 or 7 to 1, olive oil to vinegar.
4. Add 3 or 4 or 5 good shakes of Lea & Perrins sauce.
5. Stick your hand in a sugar bowl. Grab a medium-size handful and spray that on top.
6. Add fresh-ground black pepper (I'm not a food snob, but I draw the line at extra-virgin olive oil and fresh-ground pepper—it's worth it) and a reasonable amount of salt. You can always add more. Keep tasting and adjusting the dressing until you get the best flavor.

*Serves 4*

(We call this "Marsh Slaw" after my grandmother on my mother's side. My sisters called her Marsh, I called her Mam Rose.)

You need to serve this meal with beer. Not wheat beer, not ale, not bitter, not microbrew.

Ice-cold beer.

The best thing to do is to take butcher paper and spread it out on the table and have paper plates and just put the whole loaves in the middle and have people grab and pull at the food. Dunk the pieces of loaf in whichever of the sauces takes your fancy. This ain't no place for Miss Manners. This is for people you are loyal to: family and friends. They're going to like you for it. It might make them more loyal to you. Remember, this is conversation food, not Super Bowl food. Not munchies. Sit, talk, and eat yourself stupid. This food is not ancillary to the event. The food is the event.

After you've served everything, take a picture of Grandma and start slapping it around.

You don't need any dessert. Dessert is another beer. You just take a nap.

# War:
# The Ultimate Test

**In our brief survey,** we have looked at sticking and loyalty in a number of ways. We have looked at loyalty to family and friends and all that it signifies there. We have looked at loyalty to God and to country; in politics and in sports; and we have mentioned loyalty to gas companies, hotels, and hair care products. We have looked at loyalty in theory and in practice and, along the way, we have identified some people we would characterize as loyal and some people we would say were royally disloyal backstabbers. Now, I want to look at loyalty under its most extreme test and where it is seen in its highest form.

In the Bible, John 15:13 tells us that "Greater love hath no man than this, that a man lay down his life for his friends." Now clearly this is not something we have to think about in our day-to-day lives. Most of us, thank God, are never placed in a position where we might even have to consider making this sacrifice. But there is a human activity that almost demands that people be prepared to do this. That is war. At the front line, when men and women are in combat, and in the heat of battle, amidst the chaos, the confusion, and the fog of war, people do put their lives on the line for a friend or friends. And sometimes they pay that price and die for their friend. To me, that is the highest form of loyalty. The ultimate in sticking with someone is to die for them.

Now I don't mean to say that war is a great and glorious thing that gives people a chance to be heroes. It's not great and glorious—it's always a terrible, wasteful, tragic thing. No one in their right mind wants to go to war or be at the front line. I'm just saying that once people are there, however reluctantly they have been put in that position, they may perform tremendous feats of bravery that we can identify as the highest form of loyalty. They might be surprised that they have it in them to do it, but extraordinary circumstances can bring extraordinary actions.

In order to get people to go to war, all countries call upon the patriotism of their people. Americans have always honored the nation. We believe we are a special people blessed with living in a special country and indeed we are. We've talked about patriotism and loyalty to the country. And about how the country can get involved in a bad war like Vietnam.

But in the last fifty years, we have fought a number of wars that have been beyond a doubt on the side of good. The war in Kosovo has been described by the Czech president, Václav Havel, who is one of the great people of our time, as the "first humanitarian war."[1] Certainly, when we were fighting Hitler and fascism, that was a noble cause. We have fought wars where the cause has been given as one of democracy or of liberation. In war, if you are a soldier you are always fighting for a cause that your country has chosen for you. And the country itself is a significant part of that, of course: You are fighting for America. Or Russia or Germany. And sometimes a soldier fights for a cause that is not a country, but is a religious, political, or tribal cause.

No matter what the cause, there are countless examples in history of unbelievable courage under fire, the kind of sacrifice that is almost inexplicable. We cite just a few: from the Battle of Thermopylae in 480 B.C., when Spartan king Leonidas and his 300 troops held off an entire Persian army, to the Rangers pinned down in Mogadishu in 1994. You can go via the Charge of the Light Brigade in the Crimean War to the trenches of the First World War, and D-Day and the Normandy beaches. John Keegan writes of the butchery of warfare in the nineteenth century:

*Men stood silent and inert in rows to be slaughtered, often for hours at a time; at Borodino the infantry of Ostermann-Tolstoi's corps are reported to have stood under point-blank artillery fire for two hours, "during which the only movement was the stirring in the lines caused by falling bodies."*[2]

The Battle of Borodino was in 1812. During the time of Napoleon, armies moved in serried ranks in big formations as they had done for centuries. But technology had caught up with soldiers standing in a line advancing across open ground. They could be shot at from a relatively safe distance. Still, men were sent against the guns. By and large it was not a priority of officers to conserve their men. Most often it was not a consideration at all. Strategy was pretty simple. We want to get hold of that bit of ground. Here are the men. Send them in. Like the Charge of the Light Brigade, where horses were sent against positions held by artillery.

Take Pickett's Charge during the Civil War, for example. At the Battle of Gettysburg, eleven thousand Confederates were led across three quarters of a mile of open ground in bright sunshine against massed guns. They walked across the open ground! You can go to the battlefield today and climb up the tower and look at the ground they marched across. Needless to say, they failed to capture the position and suffered 60 percent casualties. As a Virginia captain wrote home, "We gained nothing but glory, and lost our bravest men."[3]

The First World War was the pick of all history's pointless and stupid conflicts. In the trench warfare of the Western Front, men were constantly ordered to charge right over barbed-wire positions and into machine guns. In the war, France lost 1.7 million dead. Of those who served in the army, 17 percent were killed. Of those boys born in France and Britain between 1892 and 1895, about one third were killed in the war.[4] The First World War destroyed any notion that war was a romantic and glamorous pursuit. Millions clamored to sign up to fight at the beginning of the war, but no one had illusions about what war was like by the end of it. It helped bring down the Russian monarchy, as one of the Bolshevik promises was to get out of the conflict.

Large parts of the French army had a negative reaction to the slaughter. In 1917, after years of trench warfare, upward of half of it kind of went on strike. They would defend their lines, but not attack, and they demanded better food and leave and the like. The various mutinies were suppressed, but for a while the French had what is described as a "live and let live" attitude toward the Germans in the trenches opposite. Leave us alone and we'll leave you alone.[5] Mutinies have always happened in wartime. The soldiers in one brigade in Pickett's Charge ran off. About 7.5 percent of all the troops in the Mexican War in the 1850s—6,750 men—deserted.[6]

I think the important question to ask here is not why these guys—the French armies and all the men who have walked away—did what they did, but what stopped the rest from joining them. As we've said before, I think that most people are by nature pretty loyal. They have a sense of duty in these circumstances and they have a feeling that they should obey an order. If some asshole officer just out of diapers tells you to jump off a cliff, you have to do it because you're in the army. Obeying an order is an affirmative act of loyalty to code and country.

But another reason people do what they do in wartime, and one that gets to the heart of our notion of the highest form of loyalty being exhibited in war, is that people also obey orders because they don't want to let their fellow soldiers down. (The same goes for people in the other services, of course. When I say "soldiers," I include Marines and Navy and Air Force people.) The largest armies can be broken down into small units like the platoon or smaller units like the guy in the foxhole with you or the other guys flying with you on the plane. At that level, a quite extraordinary level of camaraderie can develop. When lives are constantly at stake, when a mistake can result in someone getting killed, people find that they have seriously compelling reasons for sticking with each other. So most individuals, when told to jump off that cliff, will do it, and they will be confident that one of their buddies is going to catch them as they land.

This is not an absolute rule, of course. Armies are obviously reflections of the societies they represent because they are drawn from them. In his book *Citizen Soldiers* our great historian Stephen E. Ambrose, who, I am proud to say, is founding director of the Eisenhower Center for American Studies at the University of New Orleans, writes about the U.S. Army as it fought from Normandy through to Berlin at the end of the Second World War. Along with the regular soldiers, Ambrose also writes about the jerks that exist in all walks of life who were there after D-Day too. In war, they are the thieves and profiteers and small-minded "chickenshits" obsessed with the rules and putting one over on the weaker guy. These are not loyal people.[7]

But he also writes about the terrible fighting from hedgerow to hedgerow that the GIs undertook as they moved out from the Normandy beachheads. These were mostly young guys, terribly young—many of them teenagers, people who these days couldn't buy a beer in a bar. They were shot at and shelled, inching forward against an often ferocious enemy. They lived in holes in the ground that might be no more than a hundred yards from the German positions. They were dirty, damp, hungry, and often afraid. It's worth quoting at some length what Stephen Ambrose writes about the men who shared a foxhole:

*Foxhole buddies developed a closeness unknown to all others. They were closer than friends, closer than brothers. Their relationship was different from that of lovers. Their trust in and knowledge of each other was total. They got to know each other's life stories, what they did before they came into the Army, what their parents, brothers, and sisters were like, their teachers, what they liked to eat and drink, what their capabilities were. Sometimes they hated one another; more often they loved one another in a way known only to combat veterans. Without thinking about it, they would share their last bite or last drink of water or a blanket—and they would die for one another.[8]*

Now, note this last line well. This is not James Carville saying this, it is Stephen Ambrose, one of our best historians, a man who's written a bunch of books on Eisenhower and a great book on D-Day among many others.

I think what he is saying holds true for most all soldiers in all armies over the whole of time, or at least as long as there have been armies. And I don't know for sure, but I bet that the soldiers who make it through a war have at least one buddy they can point to who helped them survive.

To a great extent, a soldier's experience in war comes down to a small group of buddies looking after each other, making sure they get through it in one piece if possible. Sure the object of the war might have been fighting Hitler and fascism, but in the forefront of a grunt's thoughts were his buddies close at hand. I need this guy to look out for me, so I'm going to look out for him. So, for me, loyalty in war is far more about personal relationships. Looking after your friends in the service of a larger cause. This might start with sharing food and a blanket, but it might go up to and include dying for someone.

Let's listen to an eyewitness. Studs Terkel interviewed Second World War vets for his book *The Good War.* One of them was a six-foot-five infantryman called Robert Rasmus (his mother told him to say he was too tall to be a rifleman). He was called up at nineteen and trained at Fort Benning, Georgia. It was the first time he'd been out of the Midwest, the first time he'd heard a New England accent. A special bond developed among the guys who were in basic training together. (Rasmus bumped into one of them in the street thirty-nine years after they'd left Fort Benning, and they recognized one another at once.)

At Fort Benning, Rasmus got the flu and lost eight days' training, so he was held back from his battalion as it was shipped out. The group he was with was sent to the 106th Division, which got badly hit at the Battle of the Bulge. Rasmus would send his friends letters from the States, but they'd get returned because the guy had been killed or was MIA. He was soon in combat himself, for six weeks, of which he said he could remember every minute. In the book, Rasmus describes what you could call the full combat experience: on the front line, in deadly danger; seeing Germans get killed; stopping a Russian soldier from strangling a prisoner. But Rasmus was still upset that he had not gone with his original group to the Battle of the Bulge. Here's what he says:

*The reason you storm the beaches is not patriotism or bravery. It's that sense of not wanting to fail your buddies. Having to leave that group when I had the flu may have saved my life. Yet to me, that kid, it was a disaster.*[9]

Having started his war with a particular group of guys, he wanted to see it through with them, whatever the consequences.

There's another account that I want to talk about: William Manchester's *Goodbye Darkness.* I think this is a particularly honest book; there's no false gung ho bullshit in here at all. Manchester had been in officer training at Quantico but had flunked out. He went on to lead a group of Marines he called the Raggedy Asses. The book tells of the author's war in the island-hopping campaigns against the Japanese in the Pacific. The fighting was terrible: The Japanese defenders were relentless, and the islands, often just coral atolls, were extremely tough to attack. The Japanese were solidly dug into the rock and U.S. casualties were massive.

Now, Manchester admits that his first loyalty in this situation would be to himself:

*Short of turning my back on the Japs and showing a clean pair of heels, which would merely make me a more conspicuous target—in combat he who fights and runs away may not live to fight another day—my actions would be governed solely by determination to survive the war.*[10]

Manchester showed tremendous courage at many times. He took part in some murderous fighting: He was at Okinawa on

Sugar Loaf Hill, where 7,500 Marines fell in nine days. I think he means he would not die willingly and concedes that his primary loyalty was to his own ass.

He goes on to tell a harrowing story. Manchester was pinned down with his men behind a seawall on Tarawa Atoll right after they stormed the beach. In the third wave was an officer who'd been in Manchester's class at Quantico. There, Manchester had called him "Tubby," and he called him Tubby again, which annoyed the hell out of the guy.

Manchester and Tubby argued about what they should do. Tubby said he wanted to go "over the top"—to attack the Japanese position head-on. Manchester said that would be suicide, and Tubby accused him of being scared and ridiculed him in front of his men. Tubby said that the Japanese were killing men of the First Battalion stuck on the beach. This is what Manchester writes:

*He didn't even realize that a combat man's loyalty is confined to those around him, that as far as the Raggedy Ass Marines were concerned the First Battalion might as well have belonged to a separate race.*[11]

Tubby made two guys give him a lift up onto and over the seawall. He looked down and told Manchester's men to follow him. "Nobody moved," Manchester writes. "I stood beneath the wall, my arms outstretched, waiting to catch what would be left. At that moment the slugs hit him. It was a Nambu [a Japanese machine gun]; it stitched him vertically, from forehead to crotch."[12]

Manchester had been loyal to his guys rather than an officer giving him an order that he knew to be stupid. The officer died and advanced the cause of the war not at all. Manchester survived to fight another day. Some people in that circumstance may well have gone with Tubby. We've said before that loyalty can be very complicated. We've said that loyalty is not stupidity, and many people would say that going over the top in these circumstances is just that. It's certainly not clear-cut.

Manchester describes a trip he made in the late 1970s to battlegrounds like Okinawa and Bataan. He recalled leaving a wartime hospital bed to go back to the line. It was a violation of orders and, on the face of it, an insane act. More than thirty years later, it suddenly occurred to him why he had done it:

*It was an act of love. Those men on the line were my family, my home. They were closer to me than I can say, closer than any friends had been or ever would be. They had never let me down, and I couldn't do it to them. I had to be with them, rather than let them die and me live with the knowledge that I might have saved them. Men, I now knew, do not fight for flag or country, for the Marine Corps or glory or any other abstraction. They fight for one another. Any man in combat who lacks comrades who will die for him, or for whom he is willing to die, is not a man at all. He is truly damned.*[13]

For the men in his own battalion, men like Barney, Rip, Knocko, Horse, Mickey, Swifty Crabbe, Pisser McAdam, Killer Kane, he would do anything, including offer his life. This did not extend, as we have seen, to everyone in the army.

Let's look at a soldier from another army. The Soviet regime instilled mass terror on its own people before the Second World War. It made Stalin out as one of the great national heroes, in whose name the war was fought. But when it came down to it, the armies fought for the motherland and for their cities and for their families and for their buddies, I am convinced. In the nightmarish hell of Stalingrad, a battle that is incomprehensible to the American mind, it wasn't about Stalin versus Hitler. As a Soviet soldier and poet wrote:

> *To be honest about it—*
> *In the trenches the last thing we thought about*
> *Was Stalin.*[14]

Of course it does make a great difference if you are defending your homeland or even your actual home. And it's easier to fight when there is a cause to believe in. Many of the rebels in the Civil War were convinced of their cause. In religious wars, people do terrible things in the name of their God and they also endure incredible hardships. But still, whatever the circumstances, whatever the cause, whoever you're fighting for or against, people are, at root, going to act pretty much the same.

I think we have a good handle on what loyalty means to an individual at the most defining moment in their life. When people are stripped of their conditioning and behavior, and when it's put to the ultimate test, loyalty is a simple visceral thing. War is a mirror of society operating under extreme pressure. And under that pressure, you reduce someone to their essence, you strip someone down. When you do that, you find someone who wants to look after the other guy. Or he's looked after you and you don't want to let him down. And if you die in that pursuit, then that's the ultimate loyalty.

# Conclusion

**In law school, which** I attended and graduated from, but where I never excelled, the teaching method was to study only the most difficult and perplexing cases. We'd look at the decisions of the greatest judges: Cardozo, Frankfurter, Learned Hand. The theory was that if you learned about the really celebrated, once-in-a-lifetime cases, then somehow or another you would become a better will writer or would be able to discover a cloud on a title. But very few people who practice law are faced with the great constitutional issues that appellate courts are faced with and that we studied.

The point I want to make is that most of us don't have to go through the great questions a figure like Justice Cardozo had to face. And we do not have to contend with the challenges Sir Thomas More was faced with when he was caught between his loyalty to his king and to his church. I'm sure he could articulate all sorts of nuances about loyalty much better than I ever could. I'm not saying that you can't learn something reading about Sir Thomas, or, in my case, watching *A Man for All Seasons* on video. But he was one of the most respected men of history and became a saint of the Catholic Church. Most of us are not going to face his dilemmas, or Justice Cardozo's, or those of the Unabomber's brother for that matter.

When I started writing this book, doing a lot of thinking about loyalty, I had a simplistic view that it would come down to a particular kind of loyalty to people rather than to abstract things like your country. I thought that the kinds of decisions associated with loyalty were sort of instinctive.

As we got deeper in it and I learned some things, I got very muddled. The deeper you probe loyalty, the more elusive it becomes. There are all sorts of conflicting loyalties and complicated situations where they crash into each other. There are many gray areas. There are obviously limits to loyalty, but what are they?

It seemed to me like loyalty was something that you would have to keep pondering and reassessing. The absolutes are extremely elusive. And as you're going round and round in a circle too fast, you're getting dizzier and dizzier.

But after all of this confusion and dizziness, there are some things that emerge. They are not absolute or definitive, but they are some guideposts that might help someone navigate through some of the treacheries of life and come up with a way to land on the ground somewhere between a backstabber and a sycophant.

Now, when the next administration comes into Washington and anyone asks my advice on how they should handle themselves, I think I'll fax them a copy of these pages of the book.

1. Be careful about being loyal to yourself because that allows you to escape obligation to anyone else. In my life, whenever I have done a selfish act—and, believe me, I have been a selfish person—the easiest rationale to come up with is to be loyal to oneself, because that allows you to be selfish.
2. Too much loyalty can be as bad as not enough loyalty. Loy-

alty is like a drug that you need for life. If you take none, that's harmful. If you take some, the right amount is good, but if you take too much, that's really bad. You have to adjust the dosage yourself until you find what works for you.

3. It's instinctive. The allegiances are part of your DNA. You will know when to follow them. If a little knowledge can be a dangerous thing, well, when it comes to loyalty, too much thought can be a dangerous thing.

4. Dictionaries talk a lot about loyalty in terms of patriotism. And for Sir Thomas More it was a choice between God and king. But in the things that most of us are faced with, it's almost always going to be personal; about a person rather than a cause. Our ultimate test was: Why do soldiers die in battle? Martyrs are few and far between; there are graveyards full of dead soldiers. And we decided that many lives have been sacrificed in battle through the loyalty of comrades-in-arms.

5. In order for loyalty to be demonstrated, it has to be tested. A good example is that a used-car dealer who has a big flag in his lot is no more loyal an American than one who doesn't have a big flag. It's much easier to show up at a wedding than a funeral, to show up on election night when the other guy lost. It's much easier to be loyal and faithful when someone has done something right than when they have done something wrong.

6. Loyalty is an investment. We tend to think that to be loyal to someone means you have to give up something; that there is a sense of obligation and that you are losing some-

thing. Way more often than not, it is something that people pay back. You stick with them in a difficult time; they stick with you in a difficult time.

7. You can replace money; you can't replace a friend. I've lost money, and it hurts a lot for a little while. I have lost friends, and it hurts a pretty good bit for a long, long time. Long after you have gotten the money back or have forgotten about it, you are still reminded of the friend you have lost.

8. Let's be honest here: The better someone is to you, the more loyal you are likely to be to them. When someone gives you the opportunity of a lifetime, then you are likely to want to stick with them.

9. And the reverse is true. Remember "sticking together"? In the case of the Republican party and Washington press establishment versus William Jefferson Clinton, the fact that the opposition was who it was and acted how it did, loyalty was created by loathing of the other side.

**Nobody is ever** going to be able to write a definitive guide to loyalty because it's such a personal thing. As we said, one size does not fit all. When all's said and done, I'm loyal to what I'm loyal to and you're loyal to what you're loyal to. This is how George Fletcher puts it:

*There comes a point at which logic runs dry and one must plant one's loyalty in the simple fact that it is* my *friend,* my *club,* my *alma mater,* my *nation.*[1]

## Stickin'

My logic probably ran dry a good long time ago, but even I can see this point. My loyalties are mine and mine to own. I don't need to explain them. My fundamental loyalty is to my family.

Now, I said when I was talking about the president and me that some people wondered whether I was really serving my own best interests when I was supporting Mr. Clinton. And I said that it was not a difficult decision for me to stick with the president. But that was my choice. The president is my friend. And, consequently, his enemies are my enemies. It's pretty simple.

So we can make that Carville's Last Rule of Loyalty:

10. Stick with your friends. And stick it to your enemies.

# Notes

## Introduction

1. Richard Cohen, "So Long, Ken Starr," *Washington Post,* October 26, 1999.

## Sticking Together

1. See Robert Middlekauff, *The Glorious Cause: The American Revolution, 1763–1789* (New York: Oxford University Press, 1982).
2. Sally Quinn: "Not in Their Backyard: In Washington, That Letdown Feeling," *Washington Post,* November 2, 1998.
3. Anthony Lewis, "Abroad at Home: The Three Clintons," *New York Times,* October 27, 1998.
4. William J. Bennett, *The Death of Outrage* (New York: The Free Press, 1998), p. 128.
5. Sally Quinn, "Crisis as Ritual: When the Alarm Sounds, Washington's Establishment Knows Just Where to Stand," *Washington Post,* February 22, 1998.
6. James Carville, . . . *And the Horse He Rode In On: The People v. Kenneth Starr* (New York: Simon & Schuster, 1998).
7. Steven Brill, "Pressgate," *Brill's Content,* July/August 1998.
8. See Florence George Graves, "Starr Struck," *American Journalism Review,* April 1998. The article talks of how Starr, once seen as a great defender of press freedom for this verdict and others, was now feared for subpoenaing journalists and their unpublished materials.
9. Todd Gitlin, "The Clinton-Lewinsky Obsession," *Washington Monthly,* December 1998.
10. Mollie Dickenson, "Starr Chamber," *Salon,* February 24, 1998. Todd Gitlin mentions this article in his.
11. NBC News/*Wall Street Journal* polls, July 1998 and July 1999.

# Notes

## Sticking It to My Enemies

1. Niccolo Machiavelli, *The Prince*, translated by Peter Bondanella and Mark Musa (Oxford: Oxford University Press, 1984), p. 74.
2. Joel Siegel, "Pizza Hut Ad Slices Hil," *New York Daily News*, October 22, 1999.
3. See Bob Herbert, "Mr. Lott's 'Big Mistake,'" *New York Times*, January 7, 1999; Colbert I. King, "Lott's Odd Friends," *Washington Post*, December 19, 1998; Joe Conason, "Why Lott and Barr Hate Clinton," *Salon*, December 22, 1998; Thomas Edsall, "Barr Spoke to White Supremacy Group," *Washington Post*, December 11, 1998.

## Drawing the Line

1. David Osborne, "Newt Gingrich: Shining Knight of the Republican Right," *Mother Jones*, November/December 1984.
2. Gail Sheehy, "The Inner Quest of Newt Gingrich," *Vanity Fair*, September 1995.
3. *Ibid.*
4. "The Long March of Newt Gingrich," *Frontline*, PBS, January 16, 1996.
5. Reuters, August 1, 1995.
6. "The Long March of Newt Gingrich."
7. Howard Kurtz, "Spin Cycles," *Washington Post*, February 26, 1995.
8. Bennett, *Death of Outrage*, p. 149.
9. *Ibid.*, p. 63.
10. Jacob Heilbrunn, "Absolving Adolf," *New Republic*, October 18, 1999.
11. William J. Bennett, "What Hath the Beatles Wrought?" *American Enterprise*, May/June 1997.
12. Frank Rich, "Washington's Post-Littleton Looney Tunes," *New York Times*, June 19, 1999.

## In Theory

1. George P. Fletcher, *Loyalty: An Essay on the Morality of Relationships* (New York: Oxford University Press, 1993).

# Notes

2. Emory M. Thomas, *Robert E. Lee: A Biography* (New York: Norton, 1995), p. 188.
3. See Richard Marius, *Thomas More* (New York: Knopf, 1984).
4. *Ibid.*, p. 514.
5. Philip A. Klinker with Rogers M. Smith, *The Unsteady March: The Rise and Decline of Racial Equality in America* (Chicago: University of Chicago Press, 1999), p. 136.
6. Joe Louis, *My Life: An Autobiography* (Hopewell, NJ: The Ecco Press, 1997), p. 143.
7. Josiah Royce, *The Philosophy of Loyalty* (Nashville: Vanderbilt University Press, 1995).
8. Albert O. Hirschman, *Exit, Voice, and Loyalty: Responses to Decline in Firms, Organizations and States* (Cambridge: Harvard University Press, 1970).

## My Family

1. Editors' supplemental note: Sadly, James confirms the story. We thought if we put his recollection of it in a note, no one would see it. "There were these twenty-four-hour diners. I think they called them Toddle Houses. They had one by the campus that had this big glass window. Kids would go in there after they got all beered up: one-thirty, two o'clock in the morning. The place was packed every Friday night. There used to be this thing called 'pressing ham' when you used to take your trousers down and press your hams against the window. I guess I won't be running for president of the United States after pressing ham at the Toddle House on Highland Road, I think it was, even if I was only nineteen years old. Although if I do, that would be my slogan: 'Press Ham with James.'" We're glad we asked.
2. Misty Bernall, *She Said Yes: The Unlikely Martyrdom of Cassie Bernall* (Farmington, PA: Plough, 1999), pp. 37–56.
3. *60 Minutes*, CBS, September 15, 1996.

# Notes

## In the Name of God

1. John Cornwell, *Hitler's Pope: The Secret History of Pius XII* (New York: Viking, 1999).
2. Dean Smith with John Kilgo and Sally Jenkins, *A Coach's Life* (New York: Random House, 1999), p. 258. We'll have more to say about Dean Smith in our sports chapter.
3. Perry Deane Young, *God's Bullies: Native Reflections on Preachers and Politics* (New York: Holt, Rinehart and Winston, 1982), pp. 310–17.
4. Ishmael Reed, "Unequal Rights for Haters," *Salon,* January 23, 1999.
5. Young, *God's Bullies,* p. 202.
6. See . . . *And the Horse He Rode In On,* p. 64.
7. Robert McNeil, "Robertson Attacks Scotland's 'Darkness,'" *The Scotsman,* May 31, 1999.

## My Country

1. David Graham, who played an important role in the debate, died in 1999. *New York Times* obituary, August 27, 1999.
2. E. M. Forster, "What I Believe," in *Two Cheers for Democracy* (New York: Harcourt, Brace & World, 1951), p. 68.
3. Fletcher, *Loyalty,* p. 39.
4. *Ibid.,* p. 42.
5. *Ibid.,* note, p. 183.
6. Thomas, *Robert E. Lee,* p. 370.

## My Politics

1. T. Harry Williams, *Huey Long* (New York: Knopf, 1969), p. 566.
2. Peter Edelman, "The New 'Deal': Notes from a Clinton Appointee Who Resigned in Protest over the New Welfare Law," Alternet.org, April 18, 1997.
3. Bob Woodward, "Origin of the Tax Pledge: In '88, Bush Camp Was Split on 'Read My Lips' Vow," *Washington Post,* October 4, 1992.

4. Richard L. Berke, "For Lamar Alexander, the End of the Line," *New York Times*, August 17, 1999.
5. Details from William Greider, *The Education of David Stockman and Other Americans* (New York: Dutton, 1982).
6. Gerald M. Boyd, "Deaver Maintains 'Special' Ties to Mrs. Reagan," *New York Times*, December 8, 1987.
7. Howard Fineman, "A Helping Hand from Dad," *Newsweek*, September 27, 1999.

### I Swear: Loyalty Oaths, Hitler, and McCarthy

1. William L. Shirer, *The Rise and Fall of the Third Reich* (New York: Ballantine, 1962), pp. 314–15.
2. Fletcher, *Loyalty*, pp. 67–68.
3. *Ibid.*, pp. 90–100. Jehovah's Witnesses also don't have to stand for the National Anthem or have patriotic slogans like "Live Free or Die" on their license plates. Fletcher says these kinds of exceptions have more often gone to Protestant groups than "outsiders" like Scientologists or Native Americans.
4. *Ibid.*, p. 65.
5. See Sam Tanenhaus, *Whittaker Chambers* (New York: Random House, 1997), pp. 519–20.
6. See Ellen Schrecker, *Many Are the Crimes: McCarthyism in America* (Boston: Little, Brown, 1998).
7. Thomas C. Reeves, *The Life and Times of Joe McCarthy* (Lanham, MD: Madison Books, 1997), p. 233.
8. Schrecker, *Many Are the Crimes*, p. 211.
9. *Ibid.*, p. 212.
10. *Ibid.*, pp. xiii–xiv.
11. *Ibid.*, p. 154.
12. Harold Evans, *The American Century* (New York: Knopf, 1998), pp. 440–41, and Schrecker, *Many Are the Crimes*, p. 397.

13. Martin Walker, *The Cold War* (New York: Henry Holt, 1993), p. 69.
14. Schrecker, *Many Are the Crimes*, p. 107.

**The Traitors' Hall of Shame**

1. Review of *Quisling* by Hans Fredrik Dahl (Cambridge: Cambridge University Press, 1999), by Stanley Payne, *Times Literary Supplement*, July 16, 1999.
2. Fletcher, *Loyalty*, p. 54.
3. Nathaniel Weyl, *Treason: The Story of Disloyalty and Betrayal in American History* (Washington: Public Affairs Press, 1950), pp. 361, 392.
4. *Ibid.*, p. 382.
5. James Kirby Martin, *Benedict Arnold, Revolutionary Hero: An American Warrior Reconsidered* (New York: New York University Press, 1997), p. 428.
6. *Ibid.*, p. 431. Details also from Robert Leckie, *George Washington's War: The Saga of the American Revolution* (New York: HarperCollins, 1992).

**The Sports Section: Jackie Robinson, Pee Wee Reese, and Loyalty in Sports**

1. Arnold Rampersad, *Jackie Robinson: A Biography* (New York: Knopf, 1997), pp. 102–9.
2. *Ibid.*, pp. 121–22.
3. Roger Kahn, *The Boys of Summer* (New York: HarperPerennial, 1998).
4. Red Barber, *1947: When All Hell Broke Loose in Baseball* (New York: Doubleday, 1982).
5. Rampersad, *Jackie Robinson*, p. 172.
6. Kahn, *The Boys of Summer*, pp. 312–13.
7. Rick Bozich, "Reese's Gesture of Guts, Humanity Not Forgotten," *USA Today*, August 19, 1999.
8. Dave Koerner, "Mourners Remember Reese for Reaching Out to Robinson," *USA Today*, August 19, 1999.
9. Richard Goldstein, "Pee Wee Reese, 81, Captain of the 'Boys of Summer,' Dies," *New York Times*, August 16, 1999.

10. Newfield told the story to Peter Golenbock. I saw it in Carl E. Prince, *Brooklyn's Dodgers* (New York: Oxford University Press, 1996).
11. Smith with Kilgo and Jenkins, *A Coach's Life.*
12. *Ibid.*, p. xxv.
13. *Ibid.*
14. Tom Krasovic, "Gwynn's 3000th Hit," *San Diego Union-Tribune*, August 7, 1999.
15. *Ibid.*

## The Business Section: Brand Loyalty and Spending Money

1. For example, Bernd Schmitt and Alex Simonson, *Marketing Aesthetics: The Strategy Management of Brands, Identity and Image* (New York: The Free Press, 1997).
2. The Procter & Gamble information is from Charles L. Decker, *Winning with the P&G 99: 99 Principles and Practices of Procter & Gamble's Success* (New York: Pocket Books, 1998).
3. Schmitt and Simonson, *Marketing Aesthetics*, pp. 4–7.
4. Thanks to Veronica Smiley.
5. Decker, *Winning with the P&G 99*, p. 14.
6. *Ibid.*, p. 128.

## The Arts Section: Shakespeare, *The Sopranos*, and Andy Griffith

1. Bernard Weinraub, "Emmys Go to 'Practice' and to 'Ally McBeal,'" *New York Times*, September 13, 1999.
2. Alexandre Dumas, *The Three Musketeers*, translated by Lord Sudley (London: Penguin Classics, 1982 edition), p. 80.

## War: The Ultimate Test

1. Patricia Cohen, "The World: Trading Places: Ground Wars Make Strange Bedfellows," *New York Times*, May 30, 1999.
2. John Keegan, *A History of Warfare* (New York: Vintage, 1994), p. 9. Keegan quotes *Clausewitz* by Roger Parkinson.

# Notes

3. For the full story of Pickett's Charge see Shelby Foote, *The Civil War: Fredericksburg to Meridian* (New York: Random House, 1963), pp. 548–65.
4. John Keegan, *The First World War* (New York: Knopf, 1999), p. 423.
5. *Ibid.*, pp. 329–32.
6. Weyl, *Treason*, p. 207.
7. Stephen E. Ambrose, *Citizen Soldiers: The U.S. Army from the Normandy Beaches to the Bulge to the Surrender of Germany, June 7, 1944–May 7, 1945* (New York: Simon & Schuster, 1997), pp. 331–50.
8. *Ibid.*, p. 266.
9. Studs Terkel, *The Good War: An Oral History of World War Two* (New York: Pantheon, 1984), pp. 38–48.
10. William Manchester, *Goodbye Darkness: A Memoir of the Pacific War* (Boston: Little, Brown, 1980), p. 199.
11. *Ibid.*, pp. 235–36.
12. *Ibid.*, pp. 236–37.
13. *Ibid.*, p. 391.
14. Antony Beevor, *Stalingrad: The Fateful Siege, 1942–1943* (New York: Viking, 1998), p. 173.

## Conclusion

1. Fletcher, *Loyalty*, p. 61.

# About the Author

**James Carville, formerly an** adviser to President Clinton, is a political consultant. He is the author of the bestselling . . . *And the Horse He Rode In On* and *We're Right, They're Wrong* and co-author, with his wife, Mary Matalin, of *All's Fair.* They live in Virginia with their daughters, Matty and Emma.